■ More Praise for *The Abundant Community*

"*The Abundant Community* is a book that reminds us that our greatest strength as a people comes from the gifts of caring, aware communities and neighborhoods."

—Frances Strickland, educational psychologist and First Lady of Ohio

"Peter and John provocatively challenge us as individuals to understand the power of the individual and the potential of our work together. They also suggest local governments develop new ways of engaging and connecting residents to develop the assets available in all communities."

—Robert J. O'Neill, Jr., Executive Director, International City/County Management Association

"This is a magnificent book. It is intelligent, but more than that, it is wise. This book is the *kukakuka* (deep conversation) between two *kupuna* (wise elders), sharing stories, ideas, memories, regrets, possibilities, and hope and weaving all of it together for us. Read this book with your mind, heart, and spirit."

—Puanani Burgess, Principal, One Peace-at-a-Time

"In this slim volume there is theory and there is practice but above all, hope and a way out of the disconnectedness of our society. It remind us that the success of the American democratic experiment lies in the hands of its citizens."

—James Keene, City Manager, Palo Alto, California

"*The Abundant Community* presents an elegant and compelling argument... A powerful statement that can simultaneously enable our everyday politics and enrich our souls."

—Carmen Sirianni, Morris Hillquit Professor of Labor and Social Thought, Brandeis University, and author of *Investing in Democracy*

"This book is a remarkable and timely contribution. It proposes an inspiring alternative that pushes us to engage and reengage on this entirely possible journey of hope."

—Jack Pierpoint, Publisher, Inclusion Press

"*The Abundant Community* is both a gentle awakening and a powerful call to action. These ideas have inspired a network of community builders in South Africa."

—Dr. Louise van Rhyn, founder, Symphonia (South Africa)

"In an era when we look to professions and institutions to address most of our community needs, or to fix our neighborhood problems, this book provides the refreshing and empowering perspective that what we most need exists all around us—a message that is as relevant in Mumbai as it is in Minneapolis."

> —Mary Coyle, Director; Gordon Cunningham, Assistant Director;
> and Alison Mathie, Manager, Research and Publications,
> The Coady Institute, and authors of *From Clients to Citizens*

"We live in a world where every day many people experience loneliness, anxiety, and want. Many are hoping and wondering when the 'big break' will come. This book contains the map to the buried treasure. Locked in the secret code 'invitation, participation, connection' is the source of our wealth: our own and our neighbors' giftedness."

> —Judith Snow, social inventor and peace advocate

"For over thirty-five years John McKnight and his colleagues at Evanston have labored to clarify the essence of mobilizing communities for health. Now writing with Peter Block the two offer us the $E = mc^2$ of health. This book is destined to be a bible for public health and human services."

> —Dr. John R. Ashton, Chairman, United Kingdom Public Health
> Association, and Director of Public Health, Cumbria, England

"This book exposes what economists have missed: the core economy of community. It provides the vision and the tools that put a life of meaning and abundance within our reach and answers the only two questions we need to ask: Why are we here? And what kind of world do we want to leave for those who come after us?"

> —Edgar Cahn, founder, Time Banks, and author of *No More
> Throw-Away People*

"Block and McKnight go right to the heart of what we have to pay attention to and do if we want to live in a better world. Their book is intelligent, practical, and well crafted. Use it to help make your world better."

> —Adam Kahane, Partner, Reos Partners, and author of *Power and Love*

"This book gives us a new lens by which to see heretofore unseen limitations on and new possibilities for communal life. A useful guide for community organizers like me."

> —Jimmy Toyama, Columnist, Nurturing Our Taro Patches,
> *The Paradise Post*

The Abundant Community

■ *Also by John McKnight*

The Careless Society: Community and Its Counterfeits

Building Communities from the Inside Out: A Path Toward Finding and Mobilizing a Community's Assets, co-authored with John P. Kretzmann

■ *Also by Peter Block*

Community: The Structure of Belonging

The Answer to How Is Yes: Acting on What Matters

Flawless Consulting: A Guide to Getting Your Expertise Used, rev. ed.

The Flawless Consulting Fieldbook and Companion: A Guide to Understanding Your Expertise

Freedom and Accountability at Work: Applying Philosophic Insight to the Real World, co-authored with Peter Koestenbaum

Stewardship: Choosing Service Over Self-Interest

The Empowered Manager: Positive Political Skills at Work

The Abundant Community

Awakening the Power of
Families and Neighborhoods

John McKnight and Peter Block

American Planning Association

Making Great Communities Happen

Berrett–Koehler Publishers, Inc.
San Francisco
a BK Currents book

Berrett-Koehler Publishers, Inc.
235 Montgomery Street, Suite 650
San Francisco, CA 94104-2916
Tel: (415) 288-0260   Fax: (415) 362-2512   www.bkconnection.com

Ordering Information
Quantity sales. Special discounts are available on quantity purchases by corporations,
associations, and others. For details, contact the "Special Sales Department" at the
Berrett-Koehler address above.
Individual sales. Berrett-Koehler publications are available through most bookstores.
They can also be ordered directly from Berrett-Koehler: Tel: (800) 929-2929;
Fax: (802) 864-7626; www.bkconnection.com
Orders for college textbook/course adoption use. Please contact Berrett-Koehler:
Tel: (800) 929-2929; Fax: (802) 864-7626.
Orders by U.S. trade bookstores and wholesalers. Please contact Ingram Publisher Services,
Tel: (800) 509-4887; Fax: (800) 838-1149; E-mail: customer.service@ingrampublisherservices.com;
or visit www.ingrampublisherservices.com/Ordering for details about electronic ordering.

Berrett-Koehler and the BK logo are registered trademarks of Berrett-Koehler Publishers, Inc.

Printed in the United States of America

Berrett-Koehler books are printed on long-lasting acid-free paper. When it is available,
we choose paper that has been manufactured by environmentally responsible processes.
These may include using trees grown in sustainable forests, incorporating recycled paper,
minimizing chlorine in bleaching, or recycling the energy produced at the paper mill.

Library of Congress Cataloging-in-Publication Data

McKnight, John, 1931-
   The abundant community : awakening the power of families and neighborhoods / John L.
McKnight and Peter Block. — 1st ed.
     p. cm.
   Includes bibliographical references and index.
   ISBN 978-1-60509-584-4 (hbk. : alk. paper)
1. Community life—United States. 2. Neighborhoods—United States. 3. Community organi-
zation—United States. 4. Community development—United States. I. Block, Peter. II. Title.
   HN90.C6M42 2010
   307.3'362—dc22   2010009955

FIRST EDITION

15 14 13 12 11 10   10 9 8 7 6 5 4 3 2 1

Author photo: Ward Mailliard
Cover photo: Ann Campbell
Cover design: Seventeenth Street Studios
Copyediting: Elissa Rabellino
Production, interior design, and composition: Leigh McLellan Design

■ *To Marsha and Cathy,*
whose healthy skepticism and balanced world views
keep us from falling completely off the edge.

▨ *Contents*

■ *Welcome*   xiii

■ *Introduction*   1

The Elements of Satisfaction   2
The Universal Properties   4

▨ **PART I** *The Shift from Citizen to Consumer*   7

1 ■ *The Limits of Consumption*   9

The Consumer Way: Lives of Scarcity and Consumption   11
The Citizen Way: Lives of Abundance and Cooperation   14
A Choice of Culture   15
Neighborhood Necessities   18
Community Possibilities   25

2 ■ *What Did We Lose and Where Did It Go?*   26

The Origin of Dissatisfaction   27
The Growth of Systems and Their Managers   29
Outsourcing Care to Professionals   36
Seduction by the Promise of Satisfaction   42

3 ■ The Effects of Living in a Consumer World 46

Living by the Rules *47*
The Cost to Society *49*
The Cost to Neighborhoods *54*
The Wired Life *57*
The Heart of the Matter *62*

■ **PART II** *Choosing a Satisfied Life* 63

4 ■ The Abundant Community 65

The Structure of Abundance *65*
Gift-Mindedness *70*
Associational Life *71*
Hospitality *78*
The Invisible Structures of Community *81*

5 ■ Community Abundance in Action 83

The Capacities of an Abundant Community *83*
The Culture of Abundance *91*
The Citizen Economy *96*
Policies That Support Abundant Community *99*
Democracy and the Abundant Community *109*

■ **PART III** *Creating Abundance* 113

6 ■ Awakening the Power of Families and Neighborhoods 115

Competence within Reach *115*
Community Abundance Is Its Gifts *119*
Connected Gifts Create Associations *123*

7 ■ *The Power of Connectors* 132

The Vital Role of Connectors 132
A Table for Connectors 134
Welcoming Strangers 137
Finding Our Own Way 140
The Story of an Abundant Community 145

■ *Notes* 149

■ *Resources* 153

Pioneers: People Who Are Creating Abundant Communities 153
Website 159
References 159

■ *Acknowledgments* 163

■ *Index* 165

■ *About the Authors* 171

▦ *Welcome*

THIS BOOK IS AN INVITATION into a new possibility for each of us to live a more satisfying life. We welcome how you, the reader, bring your own unique experience and insights into this book through the act of reading it. In this way, you are creating this book just as you are creating your life, your neighborhood, and the larger community of the world. This idea of cocreation is key to a satisfying life, which becomes possible when we join our neighbors to live and create a community that nurtures our family and makes us useful citizens.

This possibility of more satisfaction through creating something with those around us is idealistic, and yet it is within our grasp. It is a possibility that is both visionary and realistic. Our culture tells us that a satisfying life can only be purchased. It tells us that in the place where we live, we don't have the resources to create a good life. That we must find the expertise from marketers and professionals. This book reminds us that a neighborhood can raise a child, provide security, sustain our health, secure our income, and care for our vulnerable people. Each of these is within the power of our community.

This power is silent on most streets where we live. However, it is possible to give voice to a neighborhood that is able to speak the language of satisfaction—a language that the marketplace can never speak, in spite of its alluring promise that we can buy a good life.

There is a neighborhood ideal that we all believe in, but it is usually a whisper. When we speak up for this ideal, our voices tell of our gifts, our hospitality, our relationships, and living by the habits of our heart.

This book gives voice to the ideal of an abundant—or some call a beloved—community. It reminds us of our power to create a full and complete life. It assures us that when we join together with our neighbors, we are the architects of the future that we want to live within. Such a future is made possible through the untapped abundance of every community, especially our own.

This is why the book concludes with ways in which neighbors have awakened to their abundance. And also why the book invites you to connect with the thousands of others around the world who are collecting the gifts of their family and neighborhood to create a more powerful community and satisfying life.

▦ *Introduction*

THERE IS A GROWING movement of people with a different vision for their local communities. They know that real satisfaction and the good life cannot be provided by corporations, institutions, or systems. No number of great executives, central offices, technical innovations, or long-range plans can produce what a community can produce. People are discovering that satisfying possibilities for their lives are in the neighborhood, not in the marketplace.

In many nations, local people have come together to pursue a common calling. They are groups of local people who have the courage to discover their own way—to create a culture made by their own vision. It is a handmade, homemade vision. And wherever we look, it is a culture that starts the same way, with an awakening:

First, we see the abundance that we have—individually, as neighbors, and in this place of ours.

Second, we know that the power of what we have grows from creating new connections and relationships among and between what we have.

Third, we know that these connections are no accident. They happen when we individually or collectively act to make the connections—they don't just happen by themselves.

We also know that these three steps, which awaken us to our abundance, not our scarcities, can often be undermined by great corporate, governmental, professional, and academic institutions. By their nature as systems, they say to us, "You are inadequate, incompetent, problematic, or broken. We will fix you. Go back to sleep."

It is our calling as citizens to ignore the voices that create dependency, for we are called to find our own way—not to follow their way.

Most all of us live in a democracy, a politics that gives us the freedom to create our vision and the power to make that vision come true. We strive to be citizens—people with the vision and the power to create our own way, a culture of community capacity, connection, and care.

Unfortunately, many leaders and even some neighbors think the idea of a strong local community is something that's sort of "nice," a luxury if you have the spare time, but not really important, vital, or necessary. However, we know from our work in communities around the globe that strong communities are vital, productive, and important. And above all, they are necessary because of the inherent limits of all institutions.

No matter how hard they try, our very best institutions cannot do many things that only we can do. And the things that only we can do as a family and a neighborhood are vital to a decent, good, satisfied life.

▉ *The Elements of Satisfaction*

People in the movement know what only we have the power to do as local neighbors and citizens. All the elements of satisfaction grow out of an abundant community:

■ **Our neighborhoods are the primary source of our *Health*.** How long we live and how often we are sick are determined by our personal behaviors, our social relationships, our physical environment, and our income. We are the people who can change these things, individually and with our neighbors. Medical systems and doctors cannot. This is why scientists agree that medical care accounts for a small proportion of what allows us to be healthy. Indeed, most informed medical leaders advocate for community health initiatives because they recognize that medical systems have reached the limits of their health-giving power.

■ **Whether we are *Safe* and *Secure* in our neighborhood is largely within our domain.** Many studies show that there are two major determinants of our local safety.[1] One is how many neighbors we know by name.

The other is how often we are present and associated in public—outside our houses. Police activity is a minor protection compared with these two community actions. This is why most informed police leaders advocate for block watch and community policing. They know their limits and call on citizens to become connected.

■ **The future of our earth—the *Environment*—is a major local responsibility.** The "energy problem" is our local domain because how we transport ourselves, how we heat and light our homes, and how much waste we create are major factors in saving our earth. That is why this movement is a major force in calling us and our neighbors to be citizens of the earth and not just consumers of the natural wealth.

■ **In our neighborhoods and villages, we have the power to build a resilient *Economy*—**one less dependent on the megasystems of finance and production that have proved to be so unreliable. Most enterprise begins locally, in garages, basements, and dining rooms. The first dollars in any new business come from family and friends, not banks or venture capitalists. As families and neighbors, we have the local power to nurture and support these businesses so that they have a viable market. And we have the local power to preserve our own savings so that we are not captives of financial institutions.

We also are the most reliable sources of jobs, for in many nations, word of mouth among friends and neighbors is still the most important access to employment. The future of our economic security is now clearly a responsibility and growing necessity for local people.

■ **We are coming to see that we have a profound local responsibility for the *Food* we eat.** We are allied with the local food movement, supporting local producers and markets. In this way, we do our part to solve the energy problem caused by transportation of food from continents away. We do our part to solve our economic problems by circulating our dollars locally. And we improve our health by eating food free of poisons, petroleum, and processing. This means that real health care reform is in our hands, not just in the hands of legislators and industries.

■ **We are local people who must raise our *Children*.** We all say that it takes a village to raise a child. And yet, in modernized societies, this is rarely true. Instead, we pay systems to raise our children—teachers, counselors, coaches, youth workers, nutritionists, doctors, and McDonald's.

We are often reduced as families to being responsible for paying others to teach, watch, and know our children, and to transport them to their paid child raisers. Our villages have often become useless—our neighbors responsible for neither their children nor ours. As a result, everywhere we talk about the local "youth problem." There is no "youth problem." There is a neighborhood problem: adults who have forgone their responsibility and capacity to join their neighbors in sharing the wealth of children. It is our greatest challenge and our most hopeful possibility.

■ **Locally, we are the site of** *Care.* Our institutions can offer only service —not care—for care is the freely given commitment from the heart of one to another; it cannot be purchased. As neighbors, we care for each other. We care for our children. We care for our elders. We care for those most vulnerable among us. It is this care that is the basic power of a community of citizens. Care cannot be provided, managed, or purchased from systems.

Health, safety, environment, economy, food, children, and care are the seven responsibilities of an abundant community and its citizens. They are the necessities that only we can fulfill. And when we fail, no institution or government can succeed. Because we are the veritable foundation of the society.

▓ *The Universal Properties*

At the heart of our movement are three universal properties. A community becomes powerful and competent when it awakens these properties. They become the source of power in families and neighborhoods. Here are the three basics of our calling:

The Giving of Gifts—The gifts of the people in our neighborhood are boundless. Our movement calls forth those gifts.

The Presence of Association—In association we join our gifts together, and they become amplified, magnified, productive, and celebrated.

The Compassion of Hospitality—We welcome strangers because we value their gifts and need to share our own. Our doors are open. There are no strangers here, just friends we haven't met.

These are the properties of a community of abundance. There is no limit to our gifts, our associations, and our hospitality.

This can all be considered a calling. We are the people who know what we need. What we need surrounds us. What we need is each other. And when we act together, we will create competence in our community and satisfaction in our lives.

We are called to nothing less. And it is not so wild a dream. It requires only that we create with our hands and in our homes what we once thought we could purchase.

■ A NOTE TO THE READER (YOU)

We want to define three terms we use interchangeably, even though they have different specific meanings; these are the terms *association*, *neighborhood*, and *community*. Here is how we mean them:

Association is three or more people who come together by choice and mostly without pay because of a common interest. The common interest may be simply to be together, or it may be to change the world.

A **neighborhood** is the place where you live and sleep. It could be your block or the square mile surrounding where you live. It may or may not have a name.

The word **community** is more difficult, but we use it as a general term to describe what occurs outside systems and institutions. It also refers to an aggregation of people or neighborhoods that have something in common. It is both a place and an experience of connectedness. When we use the term *community competence*, we mean the capacity of the place where we live to be useful to us, to support us in creating those things that can only be produced in the surroundings of a connected community. When we talk of a *community way*, it is all of the above: people outside institutions, connected by choice and usually affection, who together decide what they want to participate in creating.

PART I

The Shift from Citizen to Consumer

A CITIZEN IS ONE who is a participant in a democracy, regardless of their legal status. It is one who chooses to create the life, the neighborhood, the world from their own gifts and the gifts of others. Many who have the full legal rights assigned by their country continue to wait for others to provide them with satisfaction and contribute little to democracy or the well-being of their community. At the same time, there are major contributors to community and democracy who do not enjoy the legal status of "citizenship." We would still consider these people to be citizens because they function as full participants in what is necessary for a democracy to work.

A consumer is one who has surrendered to others the power to provide what is essential for a full and satisfied life. This act of surrender goes by many names: client, patient, student, audience, fan, shopper. All customers, not citizens. Consumerism is not about shopping, but about the transformation of citizens into consumers.

Our intention in part 1 is to look at what happens to the family, the neighborhood, and the community when we make the shift from citizen to consumer. When we go to the marketplace and the professional to seek satisfaction, something happens to our capacity to prosper and find peace of mind. Our premise is that these cannot be purchased.

Our larger purpose, fulfilled in later chapters, is to describe a few powerful and simple actions to do something about this. To reclaim the role of citizen. To move from individualist/spectator into community. To go from addiction to choice. This is the shift that will simultaneously restore vital functions to the family and the neighborhood and reconstruct the competence of community—all of which come under assault in a consumer culture.

1 ▦ The Limits of Consumption

THE ESSENTIAL PROMISE of a consumer society is that satisfaction can be purchased. This promise runs so deep in us that we have come to take our identity from our capacity to purchase. To borrow from Descartes, "I shop, therefore I am." This dependency on shopping is not just about things; it includes the belief that most of what is fulfilling or needed in life can be bought—from happiness to healing, from love to laughter, from rearing a child to caring for someone at the end of life.

In our effort to find satisfaction through consumption, we are converted from citizen to consumer, and the implications of this are more profound than we realize. This is clearest when we explore two particular consequences of a consumer society: its effect on the function of the family and its impact on the competence of the community.

One social cost of consumption is that the family has lost its function. It is no longer the primary unit that raises a child, sustains our health, cares for the vulnerable, and ensures economic security. The family, while romanticized and held as a cultural ideal, has been a casualty of the growth of consumption and therefore lost much of its purpose. Its usefulness has been compromised.

The second social cost is that, in too many cases, we are disconnected from our neighbors and isolated from our communities. Consequently, the community and neighborhood are no longer competent. When we use the term *community competence*, we mean the capacity of the place where we live to be useful to us, to support us in creating those things that can be produced only in the surroundings of a connected community.

When they are competent, communities operate as a supportive and mediating space central to the capacity of a family to fulfill its functions. A competent community provides a safety net for the care of a child, attention and relatedness for the vulnerable, the means for economic survival for the household, and many of the social tools that sustain health. If the function of the family is to raise a child and provide what we can summarize in the phrase *peace of mind*, then it is the community that provides the primary determinants of success of these functions.

In a consumer society, these functions are removed from family and community and provided by the marketplace; they are designed to be purchased. We now depend on systems to provide our basic functions. For example:

- We expect the school, coaches, agencies, and sitters to raise our children. We deliver our children in the morning and pick them up later in the day. Same-day service, just like the laundry.

- We expect doctors to keep us healthy. We believe in better living though chemistry. We think that youth, a flat stomach, a strong heart, even sexual desire are all purchasable.

- We want social workers and institutions to take care of the vulnerable. Retirement homes are a growth industry marketing aging as the "golden years" best spent in a resort-like environment with other old people.

What this means is that the space that the family and community were designed to fill has been sold and is now empty.

There is widespread recognition that the lost community has to be refound. You see the signs everywhere. Urban design focuses on community connections. Community builders and organizers exist in every city and town. Our intent is to move the conversation about community forward and remind ourselves what citizens can do to bring satisfaction into modern life.

■ *The Consumer Way: Lives of Scarcity and Consumption*

Some costs of the consumer life have been discussed for some time. We are familiar with the spiritual downside of materialism, the social competition of conspicuous consumption, the effects of waste on the environment, the ethical questions of planned obsolescence. What is not typically included in the conversation about consumerism is its effects on the isolation and loneliness that is clearly common in our suburbs and our cities.

We asked a group of suburban women about their lives and their connection with their community.

Each said she moved to where she now lives for the sake of the children. They wanted a safe place and what they thought would be good schools. Said one:

> *It is who I am now. I gave up my prior career to move here and live this life.*

What is "this life"? Listen to what these women had to say about the choice they made:

> *I live in a "poverty of wealth." I do not know my neighbors. Everyone has lawn care, professionals put up holiday lights, and relationships are formed by the ability to buy things. I learn about my neighbors from the cleaning lady and handyman.*

> *We have some conversations with those who pass by. I don't really know them, but there is some reciprocity. It is mostly accidental contact. There are lots of porches, but few people sit on them. You can go a whole winter and barely see a neighbor.*

> *We live in our backyard. Home has more of an internal orientation; we stay within.*

> *It is good in a crisis. People in some ways do look out for each other. They will watch the house, feed the cat.*

> *High income means high turnover. There is not time to invest in relationships. Home is more of a practical matter.*

> *The friends come from the school and the swim club. Motherhood is the way we build a social life. The children bring us together. There is a connectedness for those willing to organize it. I started a book club.*

We have sold our souls to orchestrating our children's lives. We don't have a life of our own, but we can manage everyone else's. We live vicariously through our children.

We are isolated and insulated in our cars. No sidewalks—we drive everywhere.

We had a second discussion with the husbands of these women. They were professionals and executives and gave their version of the good life.

We moved here to find a safe haven where children can prosper.

We have connected with other families through kids' sports; this is how we gained our friends. School is our common link.

My strongest community is with the men I play golf with. We go on trips together.

Asked if they would move to this neighborhood if they did not have kids, most said no.

With the kids grown, we know fewer and fewer people in the neighborhood. Now we get together once a year at Christmas time.

We know three people in the neighborhood, and feel disconnected.

I play jazz, and that has been a great outlet for me. I also fly airplanes. My pilot community is very tight.

Community is being among like-minded people. The suburbs are more homogenized. It does get a little boring sometimes. I want to break out, but how do you do that?

As far as diversity, it is nice to be in a non-physician group for a change of pace. [Physician speaking.] Others in my golf group are an accountant, an engineer, and a salesman in leasing.

This community is not set up for mingling with people. When we cut the grass, we wave or ignore each other, but do not really know neighbors.

In suburbs, we drive in and out of the house. It is a really nice house; all the resources are there. No reason to leave there, no sense of community. Very practical choice. Life is about gathering good resources.

I arrive at night in the car, after dark, eat dinner and have a regular evening routine. I can go for two months and not see anyone in the neighborhood.

My grandfather lived only five years in a small town in Kentucky. He walked to town every day, and at the end, many came to his funeral. Where I live, no one a block away would come to my funeral.

These comments speak of a life that from a distance would seem to be the culmination of the American dream. Those speaking have what most people think they want. The question is how to make sense of the poignancy and disconnectedness of their lives.

What they are telling us about is a culture created and sustained by a system or institutional way of life. A system life is a way of living that is not our own but one that is named by another. To live a system life is to live a managed life, a life organized around the products, services, and beliefs of systems. This is a direct result and demand of the built-in structure and assumptions of a consumer society.

In 1977, the great social observer Wendell Berry wrote about life in the consumer society, which he pinned on our dependence on specialists, people expertly trained to provide us through the marketplace what we once provided for ourselves.

The disease of the modern character is specialization. Looked at from the standpoint of the social *system*, the aim of specialization may seem desirable enough. The aim is to see that the responsibilities of government, law, medicine, engineering, agriculture, and education are given into the hands of the most skilled, best prepared people. The difficulties do not appear until we look at specialization from the opposite standpoint—that of individual persons. We then begin to see the grotesquery—indeed the impossibility—of an idea of community wholeness that divorces itself from any idea of personal wholeness.[2] . . .

The beneficiary of the regime of specialists ought to be the happiness of mortals—or so we are expected to believe. *All* of [the average citizen's] vital concerns are in the hands of certified experts. He is a certified expert himself and as such he earns more money in a year than all his great-grandparents put together. Between stints at his job he has nothing to do but mow his lawn with a sit down lawn mower, or watch other certified experts on television. At suppertime he may eat a tray of ready-prepared food, which and his wife (also a certified expert) procure at the cost only of money, transportation and the pushing of a button. For a few minutes between supper and sleep he may catch a glimpse of his children, who since breakfast have been in the care of education experts, basketball or marching-band experts or perhaps legal experts.

The fact is, however, that this is probably the most unhappy average citizen in the history of the world. He has not the power to provide himself with anything but money, and his money is inflating [or contracting—our addition] like a balloon and drifting away, subject to historical circumstances and the power of other people.[3]

What Berry describes is the life of a consumer, what we are calling the *consumer way*.

■ *The Citizen Way: Lives of Abundance and Cooperation*

We want to contrast the consumer way with the vision offered in another set of interviews. These are people, in this instance Appalachians living in Cincinnati, Ohio, who either by choice or circumstance are not encased in the consumer society. They are not the products of it or the winners in it. Consuming has its attractions, but for these people it is not the point or the provider of the good life. Here are statements from people who have a different view about the culture within which they reside.

We know our neighbors. People know all about us. There are no secrets among us.

We are surrounded with social support; we take care of each other. We extend ourselves to our kin network, even though they are not our kin.

There are people that are good looking like me. I grew up thinking there was something wrong with me. That was reinforced by systems, the military, schools. Then, when I was taken in by this community, I discovered who I was and that I was good looking.

We have wisdom, which we call common sense. We have self-taught skills, family taught. Intelligence is connected to character and morals. You can get a PhD, but it doesn't count.

We are storytellers. I will tell you my story, and if I am in the right mood, I might listen to yours.

Our faith is not based upon what churches teach. Plus even if you claim to be a Catholic or Episcopalian, you are still Baptist or Pentecostal.

We have discovered a way not to be lonely.

We know how to do without. Make ends meet. Make do. We do this together.

We take care of our own. There are no foster kids, only grandmothers and cousins.

This is a set of beliefs of people who live in a more competent community, who live in a way they have chosen, and who experience a more satisfied life than most. They are less dependent on the material culture and its requirements and call. They do not work in systems or reap the benefits of them. They think they have enough; their mindset is abundance, not scarcity. Their families have a function; they have the power to provide.

The two sets of statements are about culture. Culture is composed of the ways that a people have developed to survive in a particular place. To the mainstream culture, the people symbolizing the citizen way are considered outsiders, perhaps even disadvantaged. For our purposes, we call this a competent community and its members citizens rather than consumers, its families functional or function filled.

▦ *A Choice of Culture*

This contrast between the consumer way and the citizen way is a discussion not about a market economy or materialism, but about social and civic life. The social and civic life of families and neighborhoods. The people voicing the consumer way have constructed their lives outside the family home and neighborhood. They find others through work, schools, and vocations . . . they associate with others, form relationships, by becoming proficient in system life. The statements representing the citizen way are from people for whom the family and neighborhood is the place where their social life takes form. They are not dependent on systems or a managed existence for their satisfaction. They have become proficient in associational life.

For many Americans, however, the autonomous service-seeking family is perfectly normal, and whether or not it has strong ties in its local community is not an important issue. Focusing on the neighbors for a moment as an example, many would say it would be "nice" to know the neighbors better. But as a life priority, that ranks somewhere near the desirability of adding heated seats to their automobile. You can get where you're going without it, but it can add a little enjoyment to the drive.

So are they right? Can we get where we want to go without a strong local community? Or is it just a bit of social amenity? Many of us think it is just an amenity because we believe the road that will take us where we want to go is paved with accumulating more. We have committed ourselves to winning in the consumer economy. This is the world where the good life is measured and defined by the sum of the goods and services that we buy:

Want to be safe? Buy a home in suburbia.

Want to be healthy? Get a good doctor and comprehensive insurance.

Want to have children who are successful? Send them to the best schools and start them as early as possible.

Want to be well cared for? Find a good therapist, family counselor, and nursing home.

Want economic security? Invest where you can achieve passive income. Make money you do not have to work for.

Worried about the environment? Buy products with the word "natural" on the label; send dollars to your favorite environmental group.

Want to be happy and serve your country in a moment of crisis? Go shopping.

This belief that the good life depends on consumption is a unique worldview that is less than a century old. It gained momentum in the

1920s and became "the gospel of consumption"—the notion that people could be convinced that however much they had, it wasn't enough.

Jeffrey Kaplan, in an article in *Orion* magazine, precisely lays out the thinking that drives our life today. His point is that the desire for consumption was driven by a concern about the excess productive capacity of the private sector. He cites a 1927 interview in the magazine *Nation's Business*, in which Secretary of Labor James J. Davis provided some numbers to illustrate a problem that the *New York Times* called "need saturation." Davis noted that "the textile mills of this country can produce all the cloth needed in six months' operation each year" and that 14 percent of the American shoe factories could produce a year's supply of footwear. The magazine went on to suggest, "It may be that the world's needs ultimately will be produced by three days' work a week."[4] This was considered a problem.

The corporate world was concerned not only about excess capacity, but also about social unrest that would be exaggerated by too much leisure time. "John E. Edgerton, president of the National Association of Manufacturers," Kaplan writes, "typified their response when he declared: 'I am for everything that will make work happier but against everything that will further subordinate its importance. The emphasis should be put on work—more work and better work.'" "Nothing," Edgerton claimed, "breeds radicalism more than unhappiness unless it is leisure."

To seal the argument, Kaplan refers to a 1929 article by Charles Kettering, director of General Motors Research, titled, "Keep the Consumer Dissatisfied." "He wasn't suggesting that manufacturers produce shoddy products," Kaplan says. "Along with many of his corporate cohorts, he was defining a strategic shift for American industry—from fulfilling basic human needs to creating new ones." This means that no matter what or how much you purchase, you will always end up wanting more. This is the foundation of the consumer society.

It worked. No matter what our desire, we believe that specialists and systems can provide it. We think that

Health is in a hospital.

Entertainment is on TV or an MP3 player.

Marriage is in a counselor's office.

Mental well-being (health) is a therapist's job.

Mobility is in a car.

Housing is produced by a developer.

Meals are produced by restaurants, take-out counters, and fast-food emporiums.

People with this belief system are not a family in community. They are actually a group of consumers living in the same house. The effect is that the family and its local community have no real functions. And this loss of real purpose for family and community accounts significantly for the collapse of many families in what we call *divorce*—a word for the dissolution of a group with no real function.

The greatest tragedy of the consumer life is that its practitioners do not see that the local community is abundant with the relationships that are the principal resource for rescuing themselves and their families from the failure, dependency, and isolation that are the results of a life as a consumer and client. Their ships are sinking, and they struggle to swim to safety, ignoring the life raft at their side.

The way to the good life is not through consumption. It is, instead, a path that we make by walking it with those who surround us. It is the way of a competent community recognizing its abundance.

We, together, become the producers of a satisfying future. We see that if we are to be citizens, together we must be the creators and producers of our future. And if we want to be the creators and producers of our future, we must become citizens, not consumers. A consumer is essentially dependent on the creations of the market and in the end produces nothing but waste.

▓ *Neighborhood Necessities*

Our communities are abundant with the resources we need for the future. It is the awakening of families and neighborhoods to these resources that is needed. Consumer access to all that business, professions, and government have to offer still leaves our lives half full. Community life fills the glass the rest of the way, and this is why a strong local community is not a luxury, it is a necessity.

■ Safety and Security

As Jane Jacobs, author, activist, and icon of the importance of a vital neighborhood, wrote years ago, a safe street is produced by eyes on the street.[5] It is produced by people walking around, sitting outside, knowing neighbors, and being part of a social fabric. No number of gates or professional security people on patrol can make us safe. They can increase arrests, but basically safety is in the hands of citizens. Citizens outside the house, interacting with others, being familiar with the comings and goings of the neighbors.

Every chief of police in our major cities now has a standard speech explaining the limits of local law enforcement as a tool to keep a person or a neighborhood safe. They all advocate some form of local community organization that connects neighbors in a mutual alliance for security. Some police departments even send officers into the neighborhoods to organize local block clubs as the principal means of protecting their security.

This is an interesting paradox. We pay police to make us safe, and then they spend some of our money to send us police officers who tell us that the strength of our own community ties is essential for our safety! There is a name for it: community policing. This police message is confirmed by all kinds of social science research. One of the best is a Chicago study by Robert Sampson and colleagues that found that two factors often predicted whether a neighborhood was crime prone:

Is there mutual trust and altruism among neighbors?

Are neighbors willing to intervene when children misbehave?[6]

Of course, this trust and community responsibility can develop only when neighbors know and are committed to each other. So, the suburbanites whose local relationships are limited to a cheery hello to the neighbor, and the urbanites whose fear keeps them from even saying hello, are all increasing their chance to be a victim.

And if, in fear, they turn to the police, a community relations officer will arrive and urge them to create organized relationships with their neighbors.

■ Health

Like knowledgeable police leaders, most public health officials and hospital administrators have a standard presentation on health. Medicine, they say, is a minor determinant of our health—that is, how often we are sick and how long we live. They point out that while genetic inheritance counts, the major factors determining our health are our

Individual behavior

Social relationships

Physical environment

Each of these is closely related to our local community ties. Individual behavior—what we eat and whether we exercise—is determined locally by community custom and small group relationships. Indeed, social science research demonstrates that the most effective means of changing behavior is local small groups, such as the "twelve step" organizations Alcoholics Anonymous and Overeaters Anonymous.[7]

Local social relationships are major health sources.[8] A nine-year study in California found that people with the fewest social ties had the highest risk of dying from heart disease, circulatory problems, and cancer. Robert Putnam reports, in *Bowling Alone*, that if you belong to no local groups and then join just one, you cut your risk of dying the next year in half![9]

The physical environment includes the toxins in our food and air and the design of our automobiles. The control of these factors grows out of the regulations created by our local political action as citizens.

When we act together in our neighborhood, we produce the primary sources of health. When we are disconnected, we create business for the specialists in the medical system. And then, like the police, the medical system's leaders turn the tables back on us and say the major source of our health is our community action. Alternatively, the medical system expands and becomes more costly as our local communities grow weaker and forgo their power to support healthy lives.

■ *The Well-Being of Children*

"It takes a village to raise a child" is an African saying repeated as a matter of faith by American leaders of all persuasions. And yet, most of our children are not raised by a village. Instead, they are raised by teachers and counselors in school, youth workers and coaches out of school, juvenile therapists and corrections officials if they are deviant, television and computers and cell phones if they have spare time, and McDonald's if they are hungry.

Instead of a village, they are surrounded by paid professionals, electronic toys, and teen marketers. They are being trained to be comprehensive consumers and clients. And as they become young adults, the research demonstrates that they are much less socially connected than their grandparents were at their age. They are, as adults, more isolated and dependent on money to pave their way to the future. Recession would devastate them, unsupported by friends, neighbors, and community groups who can provide a social safety net.

Until the twentieth century, every society in all of history raised its children in villages, where the basic idea was that children become effective grown-ups by being connected with community adults in their productive roles.

Youth learned from the community and were productive for the community. They learned the skills, traditions, and customs of the community through their relationships with the adults. They were not exiled to the world of paid people and clienthood. Today, it is clear that the most effective local communities have reclaimed their youth and assumed primary responsibility for their upbringing. The research on this point is decisive. Where there are "thick" community connections, both child development and school performance improve.

Conversely, localities with very little social connection consistently reflect negative lives for their children. However, it doesn't take a social scientist to teach us this. We see around us, at every level of income, the costs of trying to pay for someone else to rear our children. We see it in gangs, mall-centered children, and negative behavior that grows because the local community has not surrounded and guided the young.

In the end, we see children who are school-smart but worldly unwise because they have not shared in the wisdom, experience, and loving care of the people in their community.

■ *The Environment and the Land*

As we learn more and more about the ecology of our world, the inter-connectedness of everything has become clear. Each level of society has its own role in preserving the web of life. At the neighborhood level, our decisions about such mundane questions as light bulbs, insulation, turning off lights, thermostatic controls, waste reduction, and recycling are major factors in the recovery of the earth. Our likelihood of making those decisions is greatly influenced by our community culture.

One sees the power of that culture in the universal norms about cutting our lawns. If we are to have similar norms about preserving energy and incorporating new forms, they will grow most powerfully in those neighborhoods with strong community connections and values.

Similarly, the common outdoor neighborhood space depends on our local stewardship. How we respect and control the development of our land is a community responsibility—a fact that our Native Americans understand so well. We see examples of the shift in programs like community gardens and community supported agriculture.

■ *An Enterprising Economy*

The neighborhood is also the natural nest for hatching new enterprise. It is the birthplace and home of small business. And small business is what provides the largest employment growth in the country. Plus it is friends and family that most often provide the original capital and sweat equity to start a business.

Many applied economists are recognizing that the culture of a local community is an important factor in nurturing the entrepreneurial spirit. Once again, in *Making Democracy Work*, Putnam has done research that shows the link between associational life and the development of entrepreneurship in Italy.[10]

A community where local people feel they are a center of enterprise creates the vision and support for entrepreneurs. In these communities, the members use their buying power to support local enterprises, put their savings to community work in credit unions and responsible local financial institutions, and encourage young people to initiate enterprises.

Local dollars circulate throughout the neighborhood, providing the mutual economic support that parallels and strengthens the local social support. Some communities have also created a local currency to provide incentive to support the local economy.

A related economic power of a strongly connected community is access to jobs. It is still the case that nearly one-quarter of American job seekers get their job information from relatives, friends, and neighbors.[11]

Strong local neighborhood connections spawn new enterprises, sustain them through the years, and provide primary access to employment. Remove these functions and the American economy will become half full, a land of large-scale institutions that are unable, over time, to sustain a local workforce and so large that they are destined to fail to serve the interests of anyone but themselves.

■ Food

One of the social movements that seems to be gaining momentum is organized around food. It is the convergence of several smaller movements. There is the health dimension of being more conscious about what we eat. Disease and shorter life expectancy are tied increasingly to a poor diet.

There are the environmental and climate concerns about how food is produced. Many are concerned about crop rotation and care for the land, plus the amount of grain produced to feed cattle, pigs, and chickens and how this contributes to hunger in the world by diverting food for humans into food for animals.

There is concern about the energy requirements of transporting food over long distances and the machinery needed to cultivate large farms. We worry about the chemicals used to grow crops more efficiently and the chemicals that go into extending the shelf life of processed foods.

As we become conscious of how central food is to our health, it draws our attention to the importance of food security. If we want to know how our food is produced, how it is harvested and handled, and how far it travels, this is best done through local production. If we want to be educated about the effects of diet and keep our health in our own hands, this is within the capacity of our local community.

Our way of producing and relating to food integrates many of the elements that are key to satisfaction. Supporting local producers and markets does our part to solve the energy problem caused by transportation of food from continents away. We do our part to solve our economic problems by circulating our dollars locally. Being an activist about food gets us involved in the education of our children. It also is another argument for community gardens, which can be a source of local income as well as the beautification and care for local, often urban, open space. And we will be improving our health by eating food free of poisons and petroleum.

■ Care

Care is the freely given commitment from the heart of one person to another. It is the most powerful aspect of our relationships. When we put it into words, we say, "I care for my family above all." "I will care for my dad until the day he dies." "I care so much about this community that I will never leave it." These words tell us that care is within us.

In the consumer ecology, the word *care* has been coopted by systems: businesses, agencies, and governments. We receive mass-produced letters from our insurance agency telling us it cares about us (whoever we may be). Our charities ask us to give money to pay for the care of people. Our government has a huge bureaucracy designed to pay hospitals and medical professionals for their service, and they call it Medicare.

In each case, they are actually providing a paid service—not care. This is a key distinction, the difference between care and service. Systems offer services for pay; they offer actuarial, medical, and administrative services. We know it is not care, because genuine care cannot be paid for. It is given, free of charge.

You can pay for nursing services for your mother in a nursing home, but she will lose the surrounding care of her family, friends, neighbors, and faith and community groups. They will become visitors to a service system, and she will become a client.

The place to look for care is in the dense relationships of local neighbors and their community groups. If they have a competent community, it will be because they care about each other, and they care about the neighborhood. Together, their care manifests a vision and a culture. And it is this vision, culture, and commitment that have the unique capacity to ensure much of their sense of well-being and happiness. This is the source of satisfaction that is complete in and of itself; it is not dependent on the next purchase.

■ Community Possibilities

No business, agency, or government can fulfill these seven community functions, because of their inherent limits. Only our community capacity has the power to fill the glass to the brim.

So if we don't know our neighbors, aren't active in local community life, pay for others to raise our children and service our elders, and try to buy our way into a good life, we pay a larger price. We produce, unintentionally as it might be, a weak family, a careless community, and a nation that tries hopelessly to revive itself from the top down.

Reversing this situation is what the remainder of the book is about. This path is very difficult. In chapters 2 and 3, we expand on the difficulty, highlight the power of the system world, and clarify the distinction between being a consumer and being a citizen. We do this with the belief that when we see the magnitude of what faces us, it gives us more choice in the matter. From chapter 4 through the end of the book, we outline what can restore the function of the family and competence of the community. If you are the kind of person that wants to skip the critique and difficulty of our current condition and jump right to the future, you can go directly to chapter 4.

2 ▦ *What Did We Lose and Where Did It Go?*

TO GRASP THE FULL EFFECTS of a consumer society, it is useful to understand two of its core elements: (1) the systems and management that have developed to provide the scale necessary for consumerism, and (2) the professional industries that have been constructed to service it. By seeing the consumer ecology for what it is, we can become citizens again. We can shift our thinking and re-decide who we take ourselves to be: producers of our own future or purchasers of what others have in mind for us.

Before proceeding, a small disclosure: For the sake of clarity, we contrast the system world and the community world in what may seem like dramatic or black-and-white terms. That representation actually is close to how we see things, but it does not imply that we are free from the grip of what we speak of. We too shop and accumulate to please our interests (books, art, music, other sorts of things) beyond what is required and keep going back for more.

So while this discussion is a critique, it is not a criticism or judgment of any of us who are encased in modern life. It is not even a judgment of consumption or its supporting institutions. It is intended to be as clear as possible about the limits of system life and what unconscious participation in it can cost us.

▦ *The Origin of Dissatisfaction*

Consumer society begins at the moment when what was once the province or function of the family and community migrates to the marketplace. It begins with the decision to purchase what might have been homemade or neighborhood produced. This is how citizens begin to yield their power to the lure of consumption.

To overstate it a bit, consumption is like an addictive drug, one cultivated not in foreign poppy fields but in brainstorming sessions on Madison Avenue. Jeffrey Kaplan gives a nice historical perspective on the shift in American industry from fulfilling basic needs to creating new ones:

> By the late 1920s, America's business and political elite had found a way to defuse the dual threat of stagnating economic growth and a radicalized working class in what one industrial consultant called "the gospel of consumption"—the notion that people could be convinced that however much they have, it isn't enough. President Herbert Hoover's 1929 Committee on Recent Economic Changes observed in glowing terms the results: "By advertising and other promotional devices . . . a measurable pull on production has been created which releases capital otherwise tied up." The tied up capital was savings.
>
> They celebrated the conceptual breakthrough: "Economically we have a boundless field before us; that there are new wants which will make way endlessly for newer wants, as fast as they are satisfied." In other words there is no end to satisfaction, or it is a way of promoting dissatisfaction as the basis for higher levels of consumption and production.[12]

The marketplace in this way promises what it knows will not be fulfilling. This defines its counterfeit nature—trying to make something appear to be gratifying or satisfying when it is not. The fact that dissatisfaction persists after the successful pursuit of the "good life" means the good life is not satisfying. Un-functional families and incompetent communities are the signal that we have reached the limits of satisfaction.

For an example we are all familiar with, take the function of the family and community to raise a child. The education of the child has been turned over to the schools. The state has taken the stance that every child must attend school or follow an approved curriculum until the age of sixteen. The moment we instituted universal education, we created a market for education services and products. Education became big business and in fact was modeled after industry. The curriculum is centrally defined. The day is broken into identical time slots, children are moved through grade levels as one class, standard tests are used to measure achievement. We even talk of the child as a "product" of the school and of the administrators, counselors, teachers, and curriculum specialists as operating in what we call a *school system*. In this way, we start early the migration of the child from citizen to consumer, from family and community life into system life.

We count on the school system to perform many family and community functions. Not only do we want teaching and learning to occur in the school, but also we count on the school system to feed our children, to discipline them, and to provide custodial care for them while we all go to work and build our capacity to fully participate in the whole range of consumption possibilities.

This is not an argument against schools or those who work in them. Just the opposite. We have loaded onto schools more than they are designed to handle. What we question is the depth of our dependency on the schools to provide for the well-being of our children. You can view the homeschooling movement as a response to this. It is the fastest-growing segment of education.

The same dependency goes for other family functions, like physical health, entertainment, nutrition, employment, mental well-being, care for the elderly, and stewardship of the land. All have been outsourced to professionals. All are organized in systems designed to deliver these functions in as efficient, low-cost, and consistent a way as possible.

The development of this consumer and service economy began as we became industrialized. We congregated in cities, worked in industries, eventually moved to the suburbs, and sought from the marketplace a wide range of purchasable satisfactions. As the industrial economy matured in the twentieth century, it was confronted with the question of where new growth would come from.

The answer was that growth would come from an expanded definition of what people needed to be happy, and that could best be purchased in the marketplace. This strategy depended on a set of ideas that might be called the *sanctification of needs*. We made the leap from being citizens to being consumers in a culture that successfully sold the idea that a satisfied life is determined first by defining and promoting needs and then by figuring out how to fulfill them. We created a larger market by collectively determining that families and communities are filled with needs that are best serviced by systems and professions. This is the essence of a consumer society.

▓ *The Growth of Systems and Their Managers*

The expanding desire for universal education, the growing expectations of government support, the medicalization of health, and above all the dominance of the corporation as the driver and deliverer of the good life—all create the need for increasingly large institutions and systems, and the management to make them work.

Systems are designed to create scale. Scale in turn requires consistency, control, and predictability. This is as true for delivering services as it is for distributing products.

Management provides the organizing structure required to produce consistency, control, and predictability. But by management we also mean something larger than institutional leadership. In the sense we are using the word here, management is a way of thinking about life, family, neighborhood—that these can and need to be managed.

As systems and their management occupy more and more cultural space, they expand the message that prosperity and peace of mind can and must be purchased. This fuels the growth of powerful systems. Powerful schools, powerful government, police, military. Powerful medical systems, powerful social service professions, and powerful industries to feed, clothe, entertain, and transport us. Powerful centers for shopping to keep the cycle going.

■ How Systems Thrive

One more task of management and systems is to maintain control by taking uncertainty out of the future, which is essential to fulfill the promise of consistency and scale. It makes the world seem predictable and wants its people to also be predictable. What is attractive about systems is that they seem to make the world safer and under control. In adopting system life, people choose to yield sovereignty in exchange for the promise of predictability. Even families and communities turn over their sovereignty for the promise of a safe and predictable future.

Control and predictability are also the promise of science. The strength of science is its ability to solve mysteries. Science knows how to produce replicability. Science adds to our knowledge with the tools that allow one to observe, understand, and control what is replicable in the world. Everything else is art or religion.

Science and its action arm, engineering, are about the language of standards, of certification, of solutions. In system life, we merge the two and call it *management science*. Science and its values are the promise of management. This is why the system world is interested in things only where there is proof.

All that is uncertain, organic, spontaneous, and flowing in personal, family, and neighborhood space is viewed in system space, and in science, as a problem to be solved. In institutional life, you hear all the time, "Don't surprise me." Consultants do huge studies of problems in organizations and feed their findings back to management, and the number one response from managers is, "Well, I'm not surprised." The world is coming apart. No problem, we were expecting it. Predictability and the absence of surprise are the foundation of institutional life.

One other idea goes with predictability: the idea of standards. Modern industrial systems are built on the ability to reproduce the same thing over and over again, whether services or goods. In the service professions, we give our desire for more of "the same" the name *standards*. Certifiable standards. Whether they make a difference or not, we take solace in this consistency.

Another example of how system life coopts so much of our thinking is how even the idea of customization has been taken to scale—it's called *mass customization*. It gives the illusion that this is just for you, even though the exact customized service or product is being offered to millions of people, all receiving the same treatment or product at the same moment.

Uniformity is both the strength and bane of systems. While we benefit in many ways from a predictable product or service, it also takes the joy of diversity and variation out of our lives. There is no reason to leave the country anymore. Once a mall pops up anywhere on the planet, the world becomes more of the same. Why travel around the world when as soon as you get out of the plane, you see so much of what you thought you were leaving behind?

■ *Certainty and Scale*

Here is the rub: Systems that are constructed for order cannot provide satisfaction in domains that require a unique and personal human solution. They are unable to provide the satisfaction that they promise because of their very nature. This is not a critique of any individual's leadership or method of operation. It is that systems have a limit; by their nature, they cannot provide prosperity or peace of mind or a life of satisfaction.

Here is how it works. The consumer economy is sustained by providing answers. The "answer" always has a system quality, because it offers predictability. Anytime you speak of answers, you are making a false promise. The more important dimensions of being human have no clear answer. This means that the answers that systems claim they can provide are counterfeit. Owning five pairs of shoes does not make a person successful. Owning the latest car does not provide an identity—that is not who you are. Love cannot be purchased, power not bought, death not avoided.

Despite this, in order to sustain the volume and predictability that systems require, they are forced to market and promise more than they can possibly deliver. This counterfeit promise of a good life and happiness is not just to the customer, but also to the system's own members—and this is its dark side and what leaves us ultimately unsatisfied.

What happens in system life is that we become the system that we inhabit. We become replicable. We are interchangeable parts. It is the industrialization of the person. The shoes we produce we end up wearing, and we end up telling ourselves and the world that we need five pairs. They fit OK, and they and we are in the latest style. And that is fine with me. I am a satisfied customer. Just like the millions of others in the system world.

■ *Suppressing the Personal*

A strength of systems and institutions is the ability to commodify through replication. To do this, they must deny all that is personal. When something becomes personal, it becomes unique and unpredictable.

The need for the system world to disdain what is personal has its side effects on who we become and on the nature of our associations. If you ask sociologists what an institution is, they would say that it is easier to tell what institutionalization is than to tell you what an institution is. Institutionalization is to take the personal out of a structure in order to maintain continuity.

To be specific: Say we have a little group that is doing some wonderful things in the neighborhood. Then a major foundation comes along and says, "We want to institutionalize it." What they mean is that we see what Sarah Lee Murphy and her sister and three other women on the block created, and what we offer to do is to multiply their efforts and design it so that anybody can do it. All Sarah and her friends have to do is let it go.

To institutionalize means to depersonalize. In this context, *depersonalize* means not just "Don't take this personally"; it is code for "We don't need the unique you anymore." Sarah Lee Murphy will have her picture on the wall honoring her as a founder, and it will be hung by the manager who replaced her.

The purpose of management is to create a world that is repeatable. But the problem with people, whether producers or consumers, is that none of them are the same. Management's task, then, is to overcome their uniqueness and "help" them to align with what the system needs. They do this by ensuring that every person is replaceable. They standardize work processes and automate human functions or outsource them to low-cost strangers as fast as they can.

■ *Making Relationships Utilitarian*

Automated human functions not only impact us as individuals, but they affect relationships and our capacity to associate closely with others. When my connection to another is personal, it is an exception in institutional life. "We don't have to like each other to work together" has become a workplace cliché.

This means there is no incentive for us to build relationships, because we are only here to produce together. In system life, we must betray what is unique and personal about us, that which is the sum and substance of what builds relationships. If consistency is the system's strength, then the cost to our humanity is a system's weakness. The impossibility of intimacy.

Or relatedness. That's why what is most personal lives only in the world of family and community. Systems and their management believe that personal relationships will distort what is good for the business: "Don't get too close to people; you may have to fire them someday. Intimacy may affect your judgment."

Systems, then, are designed to make relationships instrumental. Not affectionate, not caring, not intimate, simply instrumental—we are just here for the utility of being together. In our desire for the benefits of system life, we commercialize our relationships. We become interested in a relationship only as a form of barter. You see this in how recently the word *friend* has been commercialized. We now sign up friends on Internet social networking sites. I am friends with people I have never met. The virtual world mirrors the way in which real-world institutions make relationships impersonal and replace the intimate with the instrumental.

■ Humanizing the System World

This is not to say that systems do not make an effort to compensate for their utilitarian nature. Progressive management often invests in training and change management programs in order to bring human qualities into its culture. It uses training as a way of getting people "on board." Get people aligned, on the same page, rowing in the same direction; have them become team players; create cultural congruence, resiliency, adaptability, a lean machine.

One well-known example is the innovative approach used to create, in the 1980s, the Saturn car at General Motors. The management group for Saturn made a heroic effort to create a collaborative and team-based culture. They invested heavily in the capacities of lower-level employees; when they met, it was in a circle to symbolize that they were partners rather than in the usual parent–child relationship between boss and subordinate. And it worked. They created a pocket of humanity within the larger culture of GM. It was even good for business. They brought the car out on schedule, roughly within the cost parameters set for them, and the car was actually lighter than the specifications called for, which saved gas mileage and was a good thing. They also changed the relationship with customers, offering the cars at a fixed price—which is what customers had been asking for. They sold a lot of cars for a long time.

You would think that this success would have had an impact on the larger culture at GM. Saturn was a dream pilot project that would demonstrate that you could work in a more humanized way and still get results. What is noteworthy is that the personal, team-oriented, relationship-based culture, which we would associate with the community way that we are interested in here, had no impact on the rest of the General Motors culture. They had in their hands something that was innovative, something that worked, and yet it was so at odds with the dominant culture that the saying was, everyone wanted to visit Saturn except General Motors and the United Auto Workers.

The commitment to the system way in GM was far stronger than even the lure of better results. The tenacity and commitment of systems to a culture of impersonality and the person-as-object is so ingrained in their nature that attempts to humanize the culture are separated off, or actually discounted, as Saturn was.

Every system makes some effort to create more community within its culture. Every system invests in training. On the surface, it sounds good to develop people. Training is a noble effort to put a human face on the system for its members and even customers. It tries to give the appearance of hospitality, kindness, and other properties of family and community. Beneath the surface, though, most system training is a packaged tool to promote better management and more effective control and predictability.

What most training really does is enforce the mindset and worldview that what you are is not enough and someone else knows what is best for you. As soon as management offers a training program—on diversity, customer service, managing difficult conversations, whatever—it means that management knows and employees don't. Management has something in mind for its people.

The system's employee development program is not a path to freedom and self-expression, the keys to human development; it is a process that converts the uniqueness of every human being into something more standardized and controllable.

■ The Point

The point of this discussion of system properties and practices is to make clear the difficulty a system has in producing real satisfaction, not only for its customers, but also for its members. Authentic satisfaction holds the belief that what we are and what we have is enough. It entails the ability to fulfill the functions of living in a handmade, self-created way. Systems are good for making automobiles and fighting wars. They are good for a monetized commerce. But as soon as you create a world that ensures sameness and predictability, you have created conditions where the real humanity of citizens and employees is marginalized.

Our intent in detailing the nature of management and systems is simply to clarify their limits. It is not an argument against systems and management, only an observation that they have limits and we have reached a point where we are seeking from them what they are unable to provide. So this conversation is not about individuals or managers; it is about the physiology of systems and their progeny.

A final example: If you came to Cincinnati 150 years ago and wanted a shoe, you went to a shoemaker. The shoemaker would draw an outline of your foot and notice that the joint on your right big toe was bigger than the one on your left. So there would be a little more leather in the toe of the right shoe. The shoemaker would make you one pair of shoes that would fit your unique foot, and it would cost you a lot of money. So much money that you would wear the shoes for five years.

Then we invented shoe factories. We created a managed system that could make thousands of shoes. Now, for what it would cost the shoemaker to make one pair of shoes to last five years, we can make five pairs that last one year.

Two challenges must be met to make this industrial process profitable. This is where marketing comes in. First we have to figure out how to convince you that you need to have five pairs of shoes rather than one. That is the creation of need.

The other thing we have to do is make a great many shoes that are all the same size and shape: economy of scale. This to convince you that you are willing to wear a shoe that doesn't fit you, personally. That is the sameness.

You can get five pairs of shoes for the price of one, and none of them fit. It is the sacrifice of comfort and uniqueness for the sake of more (affluence) or fashion (identity). Shoes make the man. More shoes make the successful man. This combination of the system way of standardizing and the market way of promising is what sustains the consumer economy. As we will discuss later, this combination of a standardized product with an exaggerated claim has invaded every aspect of our lives, including most of the functions discussed earlier: raise a child, take care of health, provide a career, cook a meal, care for the old, stay safe, be stewards of our environment.

Of course, what we have done with our shoes, we have done with our souls, our consciousness, and our culture. We have five pairs of shoes, four of which we don't need and none of which fit. Plus their discomfort creates demand for more services: a chiropractor to adjust my body and a podiatrist to treat the pain in the joint on the right big toe.

▓ Outsourcing Care to Professionals

To this point, we have focused on the nature of systems and management, with primary focus on what is needed to produce goods on a large scale. We'll now want to move our attention to how human services support the shift from citizen to consumer. Human services have the unintentional effect of pulling suffering away from the family and neighborhood and into the domain of the marketplace. This strikes at the heart of community competence, and it occurs because we have given care over to the professionals.

Professionalization is the market replacement for a community that has lost or outsourced its capacity to care. The loss of community competence is the price we pay for the growth of the service economy. What I once went to an uncle or neighbor for, I now pay a professional to do. What my uncle once knew about my troubles is now a secret known only to my therapist. What this produces is a hollow neighborhood that does not value coming together around troubles. Neighbors pay professionals to process their troubles.

Psychiatry, for example, is the privatization of community knowledge about human development and madness; social work is the privatization of poverty and family troubles; coaching professionalizes our ambition and aspirations.

A friend who works with developmentally disabled people says that when he first meets a person with a developmental disability, they rarely have any friends. The developmentally disabled are surrounded by services, and therefore they are totally commercialized people.

■ *Converting Care into Service*

There are four stages in the transition from community and family competence toward professionalization and communal incompetence:

- What was a condition of being human is converted into a problem to be solved. I no longer die of old age or natural causes; I die from a particular disease that could have been either prevented with a better lifestyle or cured by better technology.

- Care becomes commodified, then reduced into a curriculum so that it can be categorized, taught, and then certified.

- What is personal becomes a private conversation with the professional. My troubles are now kept secret from the family or community. Knowledge of my troubles has shifted from community to professional.

- The management mindset takes over. Providing efficient, consistent, and predictable services becomes a matter of aggregating the deficiencies of the people in the target market.

From a Condition to a Problem

The first aspect to consider in the transformation of care into service is how a condition gets turned into a problem. An example is the young man who had a bald pate, like a monk, and his grandfather had a bald pate and his son had a bald pate. His grandfather used to say to him, "You know what is the proof that you really are your mother's child? You have a pate." It was a mark of being a member of the family.

Then somebody came along and said, "No, having a bald pate is not a mark of your being a family member. It is not your coat of arms, it is a problem. I have a salve that you can rub on your head that will erase it. Or, if you are in a hurry, surgery is possible." What was a condition is now turned into a problem that can be solved. That is commodification.

Personal limitations are part of the human condition, and they get split into two kinds. One is the limitation that can't be fixed; the other is that which can be fixed. This is the distinction between mental health, which we believe is curable, and developmental disabilities, which we believe are not. We are less accepting of people recovering from mental illness because it is considered solvable. People with visible disabilities, which we know will not be changed, are more integrated into society. In one case cure, in the other acceptance.

The point is that the condition we are in is being human. To be human means to be fallible. How do you deal with limitations and the suffering that goes with them? You can try to fix it or accept it. In general, this is a key system–community contrast. The system way, in an institution, is generally organized to pursue a cure. The system mindset thinks the human condition is a problem to be solved. The competent community treats troubles as a condition. They cannot be solved. However, they can be accepted, and the person is valued for their gifts that build our community.

To illustrate, a classic area where community and family wisdom has surrendered to professional intervention is in aging. In 1900, most people died of old age. Now old age is not even a category that is permissible on a death certificate. We now all die of a specific disease that we should have prevented through better living or detected sooner so that treatment would have worked. Death is no longer a mystery, but a failure of the medical system, the fixing system. It is a very clear example of a condition becoming a problem to solve.

Nursing and retirement homes are another professional solution to a human condition. Systems aggregate people who are aging and market it as the golden years. You can move from independent living to assisted living to nursing home to hospice without ever having to leave the property. Does life get any more efficient than that?

In the community way, aging is more accepted. John's mother-in-law was in some discomfort, and he suggested she go see her doctor. She would not go. She said she was just old and had a few aches and pains. Nothing to fix. That is the remedy she chose, as against more medical service.

She was from a traditional neighborhood in Chicago, where traditional ideas were the norm. She got through the last days of her life better than most people. She was supported by a culture that allowed her to be who she was and valued her ability to choose, even at the time of death, rather than opposed by a culture that would have forced her to get professional help.

As citizens, we know about ourselves and being old. Doctors know about disease and fixing. Doctors treat diseases; they don't treat people or defeat death.

John's father-in-law got stomach cancer, and the medical system couldn't cure it. He was living in John's home and one day got hiccups that would not go away. They took him to the hospital. After a day, the hiccups stopped. They brought him home and he died two days later.

The phone rang the day after they brought him home. It was a doctor from the hospital, a Korean doing his residency, who said he wanted to come over and talk. He said to John, "I wanted to meet you because you remind me of Korea. You are the first person who ever came and took someone like him home." As he left, he said with a twinkle, "I am glad to have met a bad American."

Curricularize the Problem

Commodification is the process of taking a human condition, describing it as a problem, and then selling a purported solution. Once a "solution" to human problems is bought and sold on the market, universities begin to teach it, certify it, and behave much like a modern-day "guild" that limits the pool of people who can offer the "solution." They elementalize it and order it. The process gets curricularized.

From that moment on, we can teach it to anybody. Professions are created and extended. When the professions have grown powerful enough to claim much of the human condition, the complexity requires a means of ordering the work, and a manager is needed. So we see hospitals once run by nuns now managed by chief executive officers.

The process is similar in most disciplines in the academy or in professional life. Health, psychology, entrepreneurship, education, horticulture, child care—the list is endless. In each case, the system way is to elementalize, curricularize, and manage. What begins as an effort to define and aggregate the competencies of caring for, say, the sick, or the young, or the old eventually becomes a system where it can be managed.

Mystify the Solution

We discussed earlier how institutions suppress the personal for the sake of efficiency. A similar process occurs in the incompetent community.

When we have troubles, we take them to the professional. The professional therapist or counselor husbands the personal and cloaks it in confidentiality in the name of care. The personal no longer resides in community, but in the professional's office. This makes private and mysterious what is most personal.

This privacy is the enemy of community because it takes the personal away. It hides and removes our secrets from relationship building among family and neighbors.

Secrets are the raw materials for a good community. Privacy is the enemy of community because it takes our personal secrets away from our neighbors and each other.

Making secrets private also deprives the community of the capacity to deal with troubles. When you take the personal and make it private with the psychiatrist, for example, it makes an incompetent community around people who have mental problems. We don't know how to deal with them. We have reached the point where we send away everybody with a problem.

This affects our confidence. If people come to me and they want to talk about a problem, I listen with total sympathy. When they are done, what I think and almost say is, "God, that is awful." Because I have come to believe that I don't know what to do about it. On the other hand, if I were living in a world where the community had to respond to people who had problems, solutions would come from my family and neighbors, from the experience they have. The culture would help me know what to do. Now we pay the pastor or the psychiatrist to take the personal problem and translate it into a private world that is commercial.

There is a colonizing dimension of professionalizing a capacity. It leaves us believing that only the certified professional has the capacity to help us with our troubles. The capacity has atrophied in the community. You do know what to do about it, but the professionalization of care has made you feel that you don't. All the professional does in the face of tragedy is listen with compassion. If you listened to your daughter, or brother-in-law, or neighbor speak of a secret sorrow and said, "That is tragic," it would be enough. That is all you can do with tragedy. But we still think it is the pro who says it best.

An abundant community and a fully functioning family is one that knows how to handle deviance, whether it is our difficult children or adults on the margin. In the absence of community connections, we do not know what to do with our kids. Because our son does not live in community, there are no neighbors, aunts, and uncles, no one to reel him in.

There is no local person that he can trust who does not have power over him. So, our children keep pushing the edges until the professional is forced to intervene. When the family and neighborhood stop functioning, the task of handling a difficult child is transferred to the school. They investigate, do surprise searches, discipline, or suspend the child. We are asking the professionals to do what we as family and community are now unable to do.

The net effect of professional solution-mystification is that my own experience of my body and psyche and my awareness of my own solutions to problems are coopted by the social and medical sciences. I have to go to a stranger to find out who I am, what is my problem, and what I can do about it. I have become incompetent within the confines of my own skin.

Aggregate Deficiencies

Once the problem is commodified and the solution mystified, the transition from care to service is aligned and reinforced by the advance of management. The mindset that accomplished so much in the production of cars has extended to the treatment of people. We think that aggregating deficiencies is the way to provide efficient, consistent, and predictable care.

Take crime as an example. Crime is one of the most visible human service challenges. Our response is to create a criminal justice system that attempts to reform people by putting them around other people who are called criminals. This is the corporate model applied to social services. It creates an industry whose growth has far outstripped the growth of our education system.

With the developmentally disabled, we create a human service system that believes somehow that what you should do with people who will never read or count money is put them with other people who cannot read or count money. The same with our youth. We collect them together in youth-at-risk programs.

Systems aggregate deficiencies in the name of efficiency. Systems and professionals promise that the institution customizes care and personalizes service, but it is an unfulfillable promise. They keep trying and trying. Management training has gotten into every group home in the United States. What they miss in the aggregation of deficiencies is that the structure itself and the thinking that underlies it make personalized care impossible.

Without a shift in thinking and the reintegration of people back into community life, change can be implemented, but it will make little difference. There has been a movement in human services in the last few decades to take people with limitations out of institutions and place them in group homes—the disabled, those recovering from mental illness, offenders in transition, addicts. They are put in smaller, more intimate settings in neighborhoods where it is hoped a better life is possible.

The problem is that these people remain as isolated and cut off from the community in these smaller places as they were in the large institutions. They rarely get to know neighbors. They spend most of their days with people of similar deficiencies. They are cared for by a trained professional and leave the confines of their home mostly to walk to the convenience store for cigarettes.

Collecting people by their needs isolates them from the commerce and affection of everyday life. The customized response and the circle of friends and advocates that characterize the community way are just not replicable in an institutional setting of any size.

■ Seduction by the Promise of Satisfaction

The conversion from citizen to consumer is based on two basic value propositions: first, that what systems and professionals produce is a set of products and services that are necessary and essential to the good life; and second, that systems and professions are a good way of organizing work and essential structures for a successful society.

The promise of the consumer society—that satisfaction, prosperity, and peace of mind can be purchased—is in many ways a romantic one. And that promise has been sold hard for a long time. The conventional view is that the consumer society is the only choice, that the system way is inevitable and the cornerstone of capitalism and democracy. To argue against consumerism is to argue against progress.

There is a wide acceptance that the best economic model is based on scarcity, that land has value only when developed, that prosperity is measured by wealth, and that our standard of living is the point. All these beliefs are a form of modern romanticism taken as fact.

■ Selling Perfection and Immortality

We hold to the romantic beliefs that a system can produce care, a doctor can produce health, and a school can educate a child. That police can make us safe, and that therapists and social workers can wash away our cares and woes. That our economic future is more secure in a system rather than a local enterprise.

Systems can create the illusion of providing health, safety, comfort, and the like, but theirs is a counterfeit promise.

In fact, all that they can deliver is order, consistency, and the cost value of scale. One reason why systems cannot deliver what they promise is that they market their promises by the celebration of deficiencies. The doctor, the school, the police, and the therapist thrive on our deficiencies and needs. Deficiencies are the love song of the system romantic. And any of us who believes that deficiencies are the point, and that systems can cure them, is the ultimate romantic. It is for us that the love song is written.

Every time we surrender to that love song, the effect in the morning is that we have been colonized. We are colonized by the belief that we are a diagnostic category; that we are a need, not a capacity; and that only a system, a product, a professional service can satisfy that need. If we argue with the producer or professional, we are called noncompliant, classified as an objection or resistance.

The reality is, human beings are fallible, and the promise of a solution or cure implies that people are solvable, even perfectable—and in the case of health care, possibly immortal. The fundamental romantic illusion is that better management and better systems can essentially eliminate fallibility, that they can "fix" the human condition. A big difference between institutional and community space is that community is built around the recognition of fallibility. Institutions are built around the elimination of fallibility—the ultimate quality-control project.

The abundant community embraces fallibility and humanness. In the domain of our private and personal life, we are intimately familiar with people's limits. Nevertheless, we trust people and have faith in them— not on the basis of performance or perfection, but on the basis of their humanity and our personal relationship.

Accepting people's fallibility is a defining dimension of community. This is realism in contrast with romanticism. It is the willingness to live with people's imperfections, which is different from a willingness to live with transgressions. We have the choice of whether to accept it and forgive people's mistakes. We have no choice about their imperfections. If we want to be in relationship with them, we have to accept the imperfection.

The human condition includes the inevitability of suffering—the loss, illness, aging, loneliness, finding meaning, and troubles that fall on us simply because we are human beings. The trust and time of friends, family, and association are what make these conditions bearable and a source of strength. A culture of compassion and support from those around us is what is needed to deal with the human condition.

■ Spin and Denial

What consumerism offers is purchased solutions to being human. In this way, systems commercialize suffering to provide a substitute for what could come naturally to families and communities. This is the more profound cost of the consumer promise, the denuding of community capacity. The institutional counterfeit of compassion and support is a two-part package: first, the spin of optimism backed up by a purchase, and second, the denial when it does not happen.

An example of the counterfeit promise to customers and subsequent denial is how systems deal with negative side effects. In advertising we are promised immortality, eternal youth, and happiness. This promise is elegant, moving, entertaining. Then, at the end, the ways in which the product could hurt us are described in small print and spoken at breakneck speed. Accentuate the positive, eliminate the negative.

We saw a classic denial when the executives of the tobacco companies stood before Congress and swore that their products caused no measurable ill effects on the health of smokers. Instead of feeling sorrow about the health consequences of their product, they put forward a positive face. In the age of advertising, we call this *spin*.

Spin and denial are the institutional responses to suffering. They are designed to keep the institution on course. There is no place for the system to allow the sorrow to become personal.

When systems lift the veil of denial and spin, either they have been forced to by law, or it is long after there are any consequences. Fifty years after internment camps, we finally say we are sorry. To apologize is to express sorrow. Systems allow sorrow only when there is nothing at stake.

■ *A Fine Romance*

It requires the foolishness of a romantic to believe that there is a purchasable solution to our fallibility. The effort to find a fix for our humanity only forces us into counterfeit promises and unsatisfying results. Often we believe that if we do more of what does not work, it will finally work. This is the dilemma of the consumer economy. It leads us to the place where, when we reach a limit and still are unsatisfied, we think, if only we had more, we would be successful or satisfied. More police, more physicians, more services, more teachers, more stuff. This is not a solution. It is an addiction.

3 ▦ The Effects of Living in a Consumer World

CONSUMERISM IS ALL-ENCOMPASSING. It is not simply an economic system; in a fundamental way, it defines how we relate to our world. That is why it can be considered an ecology. It has become a cultural as well as economic system. It impacts how we relate to each other; it shapes our relationship with food, work, music, ritual, religion—all the elements of culture. And for this ecological system to work, we have to willingly participate in the effort to purchase what matters, and we must persist at it, despite the lack of results. There are efforts to use other measures, such as happiness rather than dollars spent, to indicate well-being, but these are on the far horizon.

It is this consumptive ecological system that ultimately produces the hollowness we hear in the lives of people in chapter 1, even those who are winning at the game. When community becomes commercialized and care becomes professionalized, life is hollowed out. When family, neighborhood, and community become hollow, they lose their intrinsic value, and their members become private and overly individualized. The family and the neighborhood become broken, dysfunctional.

We will discuss, in parts 2 and 3, ways to reintegrate into the family and neighborhood the capacity for prosperity and peace of mind and a path to a satisfaction.

To create a context for this, though, we first need to describe the rules of the dominant culture and the implications for our lives.

■ *Living by the Rules*

Certain core beliefs are foundational to consumerism. We are calling them *rules* because our modern culture awards them such authority and enforces them so vigorously, with such powerful effect, that they become the customary course of behavior. If we want to find a life of satisfaction, we will need to break these rules:

■ *Rule #1: The good life is achieved through our purchasing power.*

Consumer society originates in the belief that the good life is defined by what we produce and what we consume. It rests on the belief that it is our production and consumption that create life, liberty, and the pursuit of happiness. This is why, when we were attacked by terrorists on 9/11, the answer was to go shopping.

The consumer culture has made a connection between consumerism, capitalism, and democracy. If we value democracy, we must be capitalists, and if we want capitalism, we must grow our purchasing power and expand our appetite for more. The mandate to go shopping implies that our very way of life is profoundly dependent on the success of the marketplace. As if our freedom from terrorism, the ultimate threat to our democracy and way of life, is dependent on what we purchase.

This consumer mandate is a cycle designed to maximize not the quality of life, but production and consumption. All the more perfect to consume what you have produced. Henry Ford proposed that an exploited worker was one who only made something for somebody else. It was not exploitation if what we produced was for our own consumption. The great American industrial revolution turned that around into a total life. You are making that car so that you can buy it. What you do becomes who you are.

This means that if we wish prosperity and peace of mind for our family and our country, we must believe that we are dependent on producing and consuming. The measures of our success or failure are limited to production and consumption. We want to know, how do you make a living? Where do you spend your money? What movie did you see last night? These questions begin to define us.

The same goes for our societal performance measures. The national capacity to make a living is measured by the gross national product. Our national willingness to consume is measured by new housing starts and retail sales. The daily diary of these indicators is chronicled by the stock market. When the market goes way up or down, this is the lead story. The ultimate threat of Osama bin Laden is to reduce our power to consume, which then threatens our way of life, our freedom, even our religion.

■ *Rule #2: To acquire the power to purchase,*
we must follow a certain way of life—the system way.

To succeed in this consumerist world, most of us are destined to live a system life—by definition, a managed life. There is an irrevocable link between a consumer society and a system-oriented society.

On the supply side, the goods, services, and marketing power needed for consumerism cannot be provided by handmade products or a local economy. Nor can the service economy grow if human services are provided by the care of family and neighbors. Local businesses, and neighborhood or family care, cannot be monetized at the scale needed for the consumer society to "prosper."

We therefore discount and make tangential the gifts, hospitality, and associational activity inherent to a vibrant community. We devalue the capacities of the family and neighborhood to provide their own satisfaction through their kindness, generosity, and comfort toward each other.

The good life is sold on the value and importance of large systems to amass the resources to create demand and to provide low-cost commodified products and services. We call this "progress." Large systems are an integral part of our version of the free market. What we call the free market would be more rightly named the "controlled market" or the "colonized market." A free market is actually the local gathering place where local producers sell their products.

This means that most of us spend our days working in a system, in all the managed landscape described in chapter 2, to build our capacity to consume. We work during the week so that on nights and weekends we can go shopping.

■ *Rule #3: If you live the system way, it becomes who you are.*

The invasion of work and the system way into our lives extends beyond simply hours at a workplace. We talk about all of the labor-saving devices and all of the technology that increases productivity, yet "'work and more work' is the accepted way of doing things" for Americans today, says Jeffrey Kaplan.[13] So the productivity increase has accrued purely to the benefit of the system, in spite of the ever-growing ability of non-people to produce stuff.

This is an indication of the power of the consumer culture. Despite the increases in productivity, we work more, and the work has increasingly invaded community and family space. My evenings and free time are increasingly available for work. The dining room is now an office, the bed a desk. I am on call day and night, no matter where I am. I am afraid to turn off my connections to the commercial world. BlackBerrys have become CrackBerrys. You see people talking into thin air in public places. Something that used to be associated with being out of touch with reality is now commonplace and a sign of importance.

When we're not working, home becomes a center for entertainment purchased from others. In our leisure time, we search for what we can purchase to amuse ourselves. When we find moments to be apart from the work, or system, we seek to be entertained, which means spending more time in a world designed and managed by others. We rotate between functioning as an employee, a consumer, and a spectator.

Living by these rules means you have become an active participant in the culture of a consumer society. You are helping to create it and are being created by it at the same time.

These rules apply not just to the well-off and the middle class. Poor people are just as caught in the consumer society and are just as unfulfilled as the wealthy. They aspire to the same ends. They just play it out on the streets instead of the golf course. Consumerism does not discriminate on the basis of class or economic well-being.

▦ The Cost to Society

There are four specific ways in which consumerism takes its toll, beyond our own dissatisfaction and dependency:

- **Nature is marginalized.** We relate only to nature's substitutes, and we become synthetic ourselves. We engage in virtual living, we can send avatars to meetings, and we can go to a doctor to decide what kind of face and body we want to produce. In the extreme, nature and what is natural become obsolete.

- **Dissatisfaction is successfully marketed.** We have become immune to being dissatisfied and accept it as a matter of course. The modern way of doing business.

- **Care for the whole has disappeared.** The public interest has been privatized. We have surrendered the civic space where we discover our interdependence and where a care for the whole is generated. Local culture, and its capacity to provide us with an identity, has disappeared.

- **We are slaves to debt.** The debt burden required to sustain the consumer life restrains our civic capacity. It keeps us deeply immersed in making a living, and fuels our dependence on systems and professionals.

What's more, our dependency on the marketplace devalues the nobility of human existence. We treat raising a child as a project for the schools and coaches; we treat aging and death as problems to be fixed, rather than as natural, unavoidable events. In so doing, we neglect thinking about how to live fully.

■ *Nature Marginalized*

We have claimed dominion over nature through the production–consumption cycle. Nature is there to be consumed or developed or managed. Nature is no longer to simply be experienced or revered. At best, it has become a form of recreation; at worst, it is a resource to be extracted. The problem is that simply living in harmony with nature has little commercial value, and therefore it is marginalized.

We give lip service to nature, but when the consumer society is threatened, nature pays the price. As a result, we have been consuming air, water, plants, and minerals as input for the production process. We pass on the externalized cost of this to future generations.

Implicit in this process is that what we do to nature, we do to ourselves and our capacity for satisfaction. In the absence of an intimacy with nature, we have settled for its substitutes. We do not connect with nature, but instead we relate to the synthetic substitutes for what nature used to provide, which means we will reach the point where we will no longer need nature. Nature will become obsolete. What is not needed eventually disappears. No wonder we have such a difficult time facing up to effects on climate and living species.

■ The Marketing of Dissatisfaction

Nature aside, even what we produce ourselves is compromised. We recently received a sales letter from a physician practice called MDVIP. They are selling super medical care, which means that for a flat fee of $20,000 a year, the doctor will be on call for you. They are charging a huge premium for what we once had a right to expect. They are monetizing our dissatisfaction, charging us extra for their inability to provide what used to be standard customer service.

Same with technology—some would say the most visible modern addiction. When you buy the latest in technology, the cost of the service guarantee is almost half again the cost of the product itself. They are charging for what was once included in the price of the product. At every step leading up to the transaction, they are selling quality; at the back end, at the cash register, they are selling an antidote to the product's fragility. If we were not inured to dissatisfaction, we would not pay the premium. They are telling us that the product is not reliable, and they want us to pay the price for this. Amazing.

The problem is deeper than the add-on sale at the moment of purchase. Consumption dependency is in the nature of the product development cycle itself. If your laptop computer slows down and gets clogged up, the professional will ask, "When did you buy it?" If your computer is more than three years old, its age becomes the problem. It is obsolete. You are obsolete.

We are now told that we have to buy a new computer every two or three years. They don't break; they are just not up to date. They are exactly what they were; they are just useless by today's standard. The stunning thing is that all we want is the satisfaction we experienced when we bought the machine. But dissatisfaction was built into the product, and what I bought three years ago is no longer supported.

■ *Disappearing Care for the Whole*

The idea of community abundance is about our common interest and who will care for the whole. Freedom is about individual rights. The tension between common interest and individual rights has been in question throughout the story of our democratic society. In recent times, we have answered this question: Individual rights are dominant. The public space has withered.

The public space in most aspects of our lives is increasingly delivered into the hands of the private sector. Education, health care, and schooling have been repeatedly turned over to private management. Recently, even soldiering has been privatized. The conduct of the Iraq war, and now the war in Afghanistan, was made possible by contracting with what are essentially private armies.

The argument for privatizing the public interest is always economic efficiency, unmindful of the loss to community. Care for the whole has been sold to the highest bidder; in the case of public lands, the airwaves, and the air we breathe, it has been virtually given away.

What drives the growth of privatization is the appetite of large production and capital systems to find new unsaturated markets. As the traditional domestic markets for goods and services mature, the private sector turns its eyes to the large budgets in government, education, and health care.

These markets are softened up for the private sector by discrediting their competence. We have seen a thirty-year assault on government, with the subtext being that the private sector does it better. The same goes for education, where hard selling of the supposed failure of the education system has justified commercial ownership of charter schools and public schools.

Health care is the other large market that has opened up for the private sector. The selling proposition that a private health care system is cost and outcome effective has turned out to be a myth. The United States pays a 40 percent premium for health care and barely ranks in the top 10 percent in outcome measures of infant mortality and adult diseases.[14]

Government, education, and health care, at one point guardians of the public interest, have encouraged the privatization of their responsibilities. This has nothing to do with politics or which party is in power. It does have to do with the shrinking the self-governing capacity of citizens.

■ Enslaved by Debt

The fourth consequence of playing by the rules of the consumer world is how we are drowning in debt. Debt is driven by the belief that there is nothing we cannot afford and have right now. Debt is the facilitator and lubricant of the consumer ecology. We live beyond our means and are told this is a public service. The solution to any personal crisis: go shopping.

Debt is the consequence of citizens' continuing to invest in the myth of purchasable satisfaction. We end up buying for something other than the thing itself. When I buy a car, I am purchasing the myth and promise of power and freedom, not transportation.

Our willingness to absorb the cost of living beyond our means is evidence of our perpetual dissatisfaction. Whatever we have is not enough. The debt we incur is the vehicle by which dissatisfaction is sustained. It is a hangover that lingers long after the purchase. Debt is the enabling agent or drug of our dissatisfaction. Debt is an essential part of our addiction to seeking satisfaction outside of our family and neighborhood.

There was a time when lending money and charging interest was a sin; it was called *usury*. Now we pay 24 percent interest on our credit card debt, and it is called good business. Our monthly statement directs us to pay the minimum and sustain the high cost of borrowing. Many companies make more money off of what we owe them than from the profit on what we incurred the debt for in the first place. (A corruption of the value proposition.) We will sell you our product at any price in hopes of hooking you into our real business, the profitability of debt.

On the large scale, Jeffrey Kaplan writes about how our modern predicament is a result of having been sold dissatisfaction and the fact that no matter how much we have, we need more.

By 2005 per capita household spending (in inflation-adjusted dollars) was twelve times what it had been in 1929, while per capita spending for durable goods—the big stuff such as cars and appliances—was thirty-two times higher. Meanwhile, by 2000 the average married couple with children was working almost five hundred hours a year more than in 1979. And according to reports by the Federal Reserve Bank in 2004 and 2005, over 40 percent of American families spend more than they earn. The average household carries $18,654 in debt, not including home-mortgage debt, and the ratio of household debt to income is at record levels, having roughly doubled over the last two decades. We are quite literally working ourselves into a frenzy just so we can consume all that our machines can produce.[15]

Note that these figures predate the financial crisis of 2008–2009. The burden of this debt has many effects, one being that it influences our children's decision making. College-age people are now driven by debt and résumé anxiety. They feel they have to get into the striving market to make good on their parents' investment and pay off their debt. So higher education and private schooling become participants in our economic bondage.

Strangely enough, in a consumer economy, saving is a problem to most of our measures of prosperity. In early 2009, for example, the *New York Times* noted that Japan's economy was in "free-fall because it cannot rely on domestic consumption to pick up the slack" in the midst of world-wide economic collapse.[16] In the context of community, however, savings builds local capacity, for it keeps choice in our hands. It is an indication that we are living within our means. The challenge is that savings demands patience and the willingness to postpone gratification.

The commitment to savings puts a limit on what we can purchase. It places a lid on being a consumer and places a premium on being a citizen. Savings calls for making do with the resources at hand. This includes learning how to fix what is broken rather than replacing it. Shopping when we really need something, not shopping as a form of recreation. It calls for a future orientation.

The Cost to Neighborhoods

The good life is an irresistible value proposition when it comes from every direction. Our susceptibility to the market promise comes in a large way from having given up so much personal, family, and community sovereignty. In becoming consumers, we have stopped being citizens, and as a result, the roles that the family and neighborhood play in our lives have atrophied and the community has become incompetent.

■ *Devaluation of the Personal*

An incompetent community occurs when we undermine what is local and personal. Competent community is a place where that which is most personal can be manifested. The loss of the personal connection with a neighbor is more of a crisis now because the extended family has disappeared. The purpose for reinvesting caring capacity in neighborhoods and communities is to replace the loss of the extended family.

When we weave people together in a neighborhood of relationships, we have the benefits of the extended family. We need neighbors to reestablish the personal. In the process of outsourcing care for the troubles of being human in a modern society, we have lost a space where we can be personal, be fallible. We no longer have a space where others have to accept us because we are family or a part of their community.

A community is a place where you can *be* yourself. The institution causes me to lose myself—to be replaceable or to be called a "case." When some companies fire you, they meet you at the elevator and say there is no need for you to go to your office, we will send your things home. When institutions do intake interviews, they assign you a number and a case manager. This is not community. A competent community is the place where I can be myself. Neighbors exist to encourage this. For each of us, reclaiming the personal is about aliveness and vitality. Who I am.

■ *The Loss of Care*

One way of looking at a local block or a small neighborhood is to see it as a bunch of people with problems and gifts. The job of building community is to take the problems out of the closet and open up the gifts.

Here is how this works. Before the onslaught of consumption and services, our families had no secrets. When Peter was young, his mother's family lived on the four corners of an intersection. Everybody knew that Aunt Fannie drank too much and was overweight. Aunt Rose's husband left her when she was thirty-one. Aunt Martha was sweet but a little daft. Uncle Joe lived off the generosity of his brothers.

The advantage of an extended family like this was that there were no secrets, and the gifts of all were needed to hold it all together. Peter and his siblings were required to spend time with Aunt Fannie, to tiptoe around Aunt Rose, and to endure Aunt Martha when she stayed too long and forgot where she lived. In this way, each family member was a teacher of what it meant to care for someone and not try to fix them.

Now we are on our own, with only professionalized care—and the cost to us is that we got out of the habit of caring for one another. The acknowledgment and exchange of local gifts is a central answer to this. Gifts are inborn and not subject to management. Gifts don't need to be trained into us; they are inherent. They are who we are and they cannot be taken away. They are also nearby, though often unseen. Since we cannot manipulate the gifts of another, they are not subject to external management, and therefore they are an antidote to system life.

■ The Lost Satisfaction of Neighboring

A competent community knows that we are not only individually but also collectively responsible for the things that make for a full and connected life. It is the recovery of the public interest. It is the transformation from consumer to citizen.

When we contract out those competencies that family and community have lost to consumerism, we lose the power and pleasure of neighboring. We lose the exchange of qualities that make us most human and fulfilled. When we outsource the creation of, say, civility and kindness to institutionalized anger management training programs in schools, relationship-building programs in organizations, and diversity training in communities, a local communal capacity for intimate exchange is lost. When we transfer generosity to the philanthropic world and energize it with a tax deduction, some portion of our gifts remains ungiven. The service may be provided, but the social fabric stays unraveled.

This is not an argument against these programs or processes; rather, we are saying that if these functions do not exist among neighbors, then the professional versions will not be powerful—they will be reduced to unsustainable reminders. Professionals cannot replace the qualities of family and community.

It is not that I have someone else clean my house, or counsel my son, or bring food to my housebound parents when I am on the road. It is that I have organized a life of consumer purchasing as a substitute for my capacity to grieve, relate, welcome, and share wealth and resources with others. These are the elements of satisfaction; they are nonconsumables.

Our dependency on the marketplace causes kindness, generosity, and civility to disappear, and entitlement takes their place. This is what is lost in a consumer society. It is the unfilled space. If you are hollow, this is the stuff that would fill that emptiness. These are the things only we can do.

Family function and community competence lie at the heart of the distinction between aloneness and hollowness. Hollowness is produced by the way we deal with being alone. We are alone in the world, and that is immutable. The question is how we deal with the loneliness. Hollowness is the lack of resources or competence to deal with the aloneness. We then turn to the consumer culture to fill it with purchased experience. The dating service is the iconic product for a commercial way to bring us together.

Real satisfaction, as opposed to counterfeit satisfaction, is a collective occurrence. It can occur only through our relatedness, our associational life, our neighbors, and our community. When we seek satisfaction at the mall, neighborhood and community pay the price. This is a loss, because we cannot rediscover durable satisfaction without community.

▦ *The Wired Life*

When consumption becomes the path to satisfaction, there is a powerful though barely noticed erosion in our power to be complete human beings. We increasingly choose to escape from silence and empty time. We organize our life with a constant stream of activities, work, and entertainment. Our car becomes a concert hall or classroom. Our TV becomes our primary window to the world. Our relationship to exercise is to watch sports. We are plugged into either a music player or a cell phone in all the empty spaces in our day. This is the busyness of the consumer life. Here are the costs to families and individuals of this modern drama:

■ *The Family Loses Its Function*

We have witnessed the disappearance of individual and family functions. When the family is no longer the primary provider of child care, health, income, safety, care for the vulnerable, it loses its capacity for wisdom and support. Let us take marriage as an example; it is a point made by the extreme, but the point is worth making.

In many cultures, marriage was once thought to be for the sake of the family and community. This is in contrast to romantic marriage, which celebrates the individual.

In traditional cultures, a marriage was always the bringing together of two families. It was not you or me, it was us. The prototype was the royal marriage: The bride and groom were not individuals; they each represented a family, a kin group, even a country. The traditional idea of marriage, therefore, was to connect or sustain your community. Your identities were formed as members of a community rather than as two free-floating individuals.

In contrast to this, romantic marriage developed in Europe in the age of chivalry. That is when the idea of two individuals marrying was born. The purpose of marriage turned away from the tribe to the self. Individual freedom was ushered in on the rails of romantic love. The loss of a group identity was a casualty. It broke people away from the controls and bonds of their family and group. In Scotland, a man without a clan was called a "broken man." Individualism came in the side door and broke the communal bonds.

The disappearance of arranged marriage is an extreme example of how families have lost many of their functions in the shift from familial and communal tradition to individualism and consumption. Other costs to family function in a system and consumer world relate to birth and death. In these ritual moments of life, we have increasingly turned to the professionals: grief counselors, professionally managed showers, hospice run by the health industry, and hospital births. The celebration and sorrow of the family occurs in a context provided by the professionals.

As the joke goes, how many specialists does it take to raise a family in a consumer world? Now we need health specialists, SAT coaches, physical trainers, financial advisors, day care, and career coaches. What was once an extended family has become a meeting of clients and their professionals. The personal capacities of the family are made obsolete.

■ *Work and Consumption Replace Leisure and Community*

The age of automation and mass production is always justified by how much labor is saved. Home innovations like the dishwasher and food processor were heralded under the banner of freeing up more time for leisure, more time with the children, the additional time the adults could spend together. The pursuit of leisure is a central argument in creating new needs and therefore new demand. So what happened to that leisure?

"Today work and more work is the accepted way of doing things," observes Jeffrey Kaplan. "If anything, improvements to the labor-saving machinery since the 1920s have intensified the trend. Machines *can* save labor, but only if they go idle when we possess enough of what they can produce. In other words, the machinery offers us an opportunity to work less, an opportunity that as a society we have chosen not to take. Instead, we have allowed the owners of those machines to define their purpose: not reduction of labor, but 'higher productivity'—and with it the imperative to consume virtually everything that the machinery can possibly produce."[17]

The shape of the workday, how long and how demanding it is, has forever been a tradeoff between the family, the community, and the workplace. Few things impact the family and community competence more than the construction and requirements of the workday. The institution has needs for low-cost labor, long hours for more productivity, and willing compliance. The family and the community require time, energy, and space to associate. Who wins?

You can measure part of the cost of living in a consumer world by tracking the expansion and contraction of the workday over time. For example, in 1930, cereal industry pioneer W. K. Kellogg innovated the six-hour workday.[18] As Kaplan tells it, Kellogg thought to take these new opportunities that labor-saving machines provided, and instead of evermore involving people in the production and consumer treadmill, he initiated the thirty-hour workweek. Six hours a day for five days a week. He wanted to use the advantage of the machine to accrue to a fuller life outside of work for employees. His goal was not to eat people up in consumption and production. He chose to make room for community space, for family functions and conviviality with others.

Kellogg did this for two reasons. First, he saw that four six-hour shifts a day instead of three eight-hour shifts would give work and paychecks to three hundred more families. The other reason was that this arrangement would give people time for their families and fulfilling their civic responsibilities.

When he died, the managers eventually went back to the eight-hour day. So much for the family and civic engagement that had made Kellogg unique.

■ *The Capacity for Thought and Surprise Atrophies*

Another price we pay for living in a consumer world is that we end up purchasing experiences rather than actively producing them. We have become spectators. In the consumer ecology, you substitute purchasing something for the experience and satisfaction of creating something.

Being a spectator—electrified, constantly distracted—means that we no longer require thoughts of our own. Instead of thinking our own thoughts, we rent or purchase the thoughts of others. Every time we watch television, we let someone else decide what we are thinking about. Do this long enough and the mind becomes colonized. The implications for democracy are obvious.

Over time, we lose the competence to have a new thought and with it the experience of adventure or surprise. My wish for safety in the world, yielding sovereignty to my boss, living to another's way, affects my capacity to be open to an experience or thought that I have not had before. How often do you hear people comment on what a unique experience it is to have time to think?

This is true even in places of higher learning. A professor friend was having lunch with his dean. The dean said that he had been reading the anonymous student feedback forms about the professor and noticed one thing different about the student evaluations this professor had received. When asked what was unique about the professor's course, the dean said, the students answered that they had engaged in "thinking." None of the other faculty member evaluations said that.

The dean leaned forward, looked around to make sure no one was listening, and asked, "How do you get them to think?" Thought, even in higher education, has become the exception, a rarity.

What are students doing if they are not thinking? Consuming. If you are a professor in a college classroom, you are in a room not of learners but of young people just sitting there as total consumers. They do not show up to learn; they show up for a résumé that will get them a good enough job to pay off their educational debt and provide enough extra for a good consumer life.

Instead of valuing education, they are consumers interested in information. Information is the booby prize in education. The culture of the university is no longer a place for education; it is a terminal to pass through in order to get somewhere. It is a high-level vocational education. It is a credential. It has replaced the creation of learning with the consumption of instruction.

■ Boredom: What an Interesting Subject

Boredom—or more accurately the fear of boredom—is another side effect of consumption. Once I become a consumer, the world immediately around me quickly becomes predictable and boring, and the only path to excitement is to go shopping. I am bored with myself, so I need something more. Boredom is a symptom of living in a consumer world. Entertainment and consumption are its cure.

This means that I become sedentary, passive. The competence to be with myself has disappeared. I do not know how to love my world and have it be enough. When I say that I am bored, the truth is that I have become boring. This is reinforced by the system world's demand for repetition and predictability.

Younger people, with the future at their fingertips, especially feel that the world around them is boring. At a local college student center, along the main steps into the cafeteria is a twenty-foot-long wall full of leaflets and flyers posted about stuff going on. Yet one of the complaints that come up fairly frequently among students is that there is nothing to do. How could that be? They are inundated with pleas to do stuff on this wall. Possibilities of every kind, and yet they are bored.

Everything on that wall requires something of you: You have to learn something, sign up for something, apply for something, commit to something. That's not entertainment. When we are bored, we want to be entertained, which creates a wide opening for technological solutions to all life's activities.

▓ *The Heart of the Matter*

Stated simply, the price we pay for living in a consumer world, for becoming consumers rather than citizens, is living a dissatisfied life. An incomplete life. A life where the harder we try, the more hollow it becomes. Individuals become useless, families lose their function, neighborhoods lose their competence. We are then left to purchase what we might have chosen to produce.

The fallacy of the consumer model is the notion that what we are seeking is, in fact, obtainable in the marketplace. While we may know intellectually that a satisfied life cannot be purchased, we have an economy whose very success counts on our dissatisfaction and is dependent on our continuous effort to make the purchase. The dominant cultural reality for developed countries is that once we become a customer in the consumer society, our dissatisfaction is guaranteed. "Customer satisfaction" has become a euphemism; it is a counterfeit promise.

PART II

Choosing
a Satisfied Life

WE SHIFT HERE FROM critique to possibility. We want to explore how a competent community, one willing to capitalize on its abundance, has the ability to create satisfaction and cure our addiction to consumption.

Community has a job to do, and that is to create conditions where individuals and families can perform certain functions. These functions are to educate a child, sustain a healthy body, have a safe street, participate in a local economy, care for the land, be smart in its relationship to food, and welcome those on the margin. The premise is that when our communities become competent, we will not be dependent on the marketplace to achieve our most precious ends.

Some might read this as a belief that becoming an effective, competent community is merely a return to the past. They are partly correct. The experience of millions of our predecessors, through time, led them to create cultures that sustained community life. These community cultures included both the wisdom and errors of our elders. It is, however, the wisdom of those community cultures that is our priceless legacy. It represents the ways that our experimenting ancestors found to nurture and sustain a life of mutual dependency.

The consumer society has stripped away the wisdom of these ways. Without that culture and community wisdom, we are naked in the storm, with families often defenseless, overwhelmed, fearful, and divorcing; neighbors suspicious; colleagues as competitors. There seems to be nothing to do in response but to try to buy our way out.

While we need to build on the cultural wisdom of the past, we can leave behind those practices that were not sustaining. Too often, traditional communities have excluded some. This is why we place hospitality at the center of newly activated communities. Similarly, traditional communities too often relegated some members to a subordinate place. That is why we have emphasized that every member of the community has gifts to give and that every gift is uniquely valuable and needed.

Working from the foundation of our historic knowledge of a community culture, we must be the current designers and builders of a community that satisfies and sustains. It is our good fortune that the basic building blocks surround us. That is why our future is, in fact, so hopeful.

■   CHOOSING A SATISFIED LIFE

Visit our website: **http://www.abundantcommunity.com.**

This is a site whose first commitment is to action. A place to find others who are like you or aren't. We are committed to learning and to supporting the movement toward local living. It is a site based on welcoming, gift-mindedness, strong association, and communities that work. We have created a website for and with you. There are four parts of the site to check out:

Toolkit. A toolkit to help you put these ideas to work. This includes methods for getting started, discovering gifts, making connections, learning from each other, and tracking the connections.

Where It Is Working. Studies, research, and transformational efforts under way. Efforts to create a new narrative for our communities based on gifts and hospitality.

Commentary. Blogs and podcasts from John McKnight and Peter Block. Commentaries from a wide network of friends who are changing our thinking and the world. Space for the thoughts and experiences of connectors, activists, and citizens. Book reviews. Especially ideas that you might not have discovered yet.

Events. Abundant Community gatherings. Local meetings of people interested in these ideas. National calendar of presentations, workshops, and meetings.

We want to hear from you. Go to the website:
http://www.abundantcommunity.com.

---

4 ▦ The Abundant Community

THE LIMITS OF SATISFACTION come from the fact that the current marketplace/service economy and its systems and institutions promise to provide answers to "problems" that are in fact the human condition. The real cost of systems is the dependency they create on illusory answers. System answers, even if they do seem to satisfy, are addictions because system satisfaction has such a short shelf life.

▦ The Structure of Abundance

An abundant community is not organized the system way—there is no interest in consistency, uniformity, and replaceable parts. Abundance is about the variety of gifts and what is most personal and idiosyncratic to families and neighborhoods. A competent community, one that takes advantage of its abundance, admits the realities of the human condition and the truth of the decay, restoration, and growth processes that are a part of every living system. Variety, uniqueness, and appreciation for the one-of-a-kind are its essence.

Where the consumer society breeds individualism and its effects of entitlement and self-interest, an abundant community is marked by a collective accountability that can be created only in relationship to other people.

■

This is not to idealize community, for it can also be insular, exclusive, and divisive. But at a minimum, it holds the possibility of satisfaction in fulfilling the functions most important to us.

■ The Tenets of Abundance

A community that has the capacity to support lives of satisfaction holds a different set of beliefs than those the consumer economy teaches us. The abundant community has basic tenets:

- **What we have is enough.** We value what we have and find it satisfying. This is true about who we are personally and with respect to material goods. We do not need to operate on the half-full glass of scarcity to give value to things or qualities. We are more interested in abundance.

- **We have the capacity to provide what we need in the face of the human condition.** We believe that this family and neighborhood have the capacity to collectively handle an uncertain future and to endure and transcend whatever faces us. We can imagine creating together a future beyond this moment. We can learn how to make visible and harvest what up to now has been invisible and treated as though it were scarce.

- **We organize our world in a context of cooperation and satisfaction.** We do not need competition to motivate our children or ourselves. A productive economy does not need to be competitive. Association life can cooperatively produce what systems have been selling.

- **We are responsible for each other.** This is the meaning of community. We take seriously the idealistic notion that our future is dependent on each of us and if one of us is not free, or valued, or participating in a full life, then these are not possible for any of us.

- **We live with the reality of the human condition.** We understand what we can and cannot do. Sorrow, aging, illness, celebration, fallibility, failure, misfortune, and joy are natural and inevitable. Life is not a problem to be solved or services to be obtained.

Two things occur when community competence springs from these beliefs. The first is that a competent community is the most likely means of *preventing*, in the first place, those dissatisfactions for which the marketplace says you need answers.

Second, a competent community builds within the family and neighborhood the power to *provide* for themselves much of what systems and consumerism would have us purchase.

A brief example: The reason why many young people have so many "problems" that need servicing is that they are raised without a culture of community where they are a part of something. They are raised with nothing useful to do, no purpose. The teenage years are difficult under any conditions, but are made more so when teenagers are not needed. In the absence of purpose, they search for the belonging found in social networking. For youth, the peer group is a substitute for the community of family and neighborhood. Their friends mean the world to them in the absence of community.

The challenge is that everyone in that world is seventeen years old. That is what gangs are. The "youth problem" is a glaring result of not being raised in a community. It is a product of being taught only by professionals and raised in a context of consumption, not community. Why else would they go to war over a pair of sneakers?

■ *Community Properties and Capacities*

Building community is more than occasional, tangible events like holding picnics, constructing a neighborhood park together, or doing a group service project. It involves the more fundamental tasks of rearing a child, promoting health, and keeping the streets safe. To fulfill these functions in a satisfying way, a community needs certain *properties*. They are the organizing principles for achieving competence.

A competent community has three properties:

Focus on the gifts of its members.

Nurture associational life.

Offer hospitality, the welcoming of strangers.

In turn, these collective properties create the communal conditions for the emergence in families and neighborhoods of certain *capacities*. These are the capacities:

Kindness

Generosity

Cooperation

Forgiveness

Acceptance of fallibility

Mystery

The combination of these properties and capacities is a collective way of being that is needed for families and neighborhoods to fulfill their functions with respect to youth, safety, health, prosperity, and other elements of satisfaction. When we make these properties and capacities more vivid and possible, it opens the way to a life of satisfaction.

■ *Origins in Human Nature*

The question, of course, is how do we achieve this? Where do these properties and capacities of competent communities come from? Here is how it works:

- The properties and capacities are abundant and exist as a potential in everybody.

- They await a nurturing context in which to be manifested.

- When they are manifested, it is evidence that a community has become competent.

- When community becomes competent, families and neighborhoods produce satisfaction.

The shift we seek begins when we declare that the properties and capacities that make up a competent community exist in human nature. These properties and capacities are in everybody, to greater or lesser degrees. This gives us another way to think about the power of our community: It holds the power to utilize the diversity that already exists within. I have courage and you have vision; therefore, we need each other. Because all my courage, without your vision, won't create anything. Without my courage, your vision is useless. Families and neighborhoods become powerful when gifts are combined.

Community competence allows our collective gifts and sorrows to become community knowledge. This is one way that community makes personal what consumption depersonalizes. All stereotyping, standardizing, generalizing in the system world is depersonalization of people. An abundant community creates the re-personalization of people.

What is personal is the uniqueness of individuals within the family and neighborhood. A competent community is the place where I can be myself by sharing my unique gifts and revealing my unique sorrows. It is where one fully emerges as one of a kind, which some call *individuation*. This individuation can emerge only in the context of hospitality, in association with others, based on our gifts; and if the community does not surround us like that, we will never fully become who we are. Our abundance will remain invisible.

There is a distinction here between what is personal and what is private. We are advocating for the personal; we are not advocating for privacy. Bringing into families and neighborhoods what is personal calls for us to move away from privacy. Privacy is the domain of professionalized services. Privacy—not letting others know your troubles—undermines the community capacity to join our lives and give them meaning.

■ Sorrows No Longer Secret

We discover the abundance of our community not only when our gifts are acknowledged, but also when our sorrows are revealed. We make them public. They become community knowledge. Making our gifts and sorrows explicit makes them available for sharing. The range and variety of the sorrows we bear gives us the fuel for community and connectedness.

This means that community competence depends on our willingness to share with others what is most intimate and personal. The job of building community is to take the personal problems and abilities out of the closet. The single father down the block goes to his neighbor across the street to talk when his teenage daughter runs away. The Irish family next door holds a wake for friends and family instead of calling in the bereavement specialists. Sharing what is personal makes the consumer service obsolete.

This is a key entry point in awakening the power of families and neighborhoods. It is an answer to the conspiracy of secrecy in our families. It is the way a village raises a child. Many in the neighborhood know our children, their gifts, and their propensity for trouble, and so many eyes are watching out for them. Sharing the personal is how the consumer cycle is broken. When we disclose a secret, others now have the information and know-how to use their gifts to deal with it. At this moment, the restoration of community competence has begun.

In disclosing, not only are we getting help, but we are establishing a pattern for how we might deal with the human condition of our community. This is a political act in the best sense—reclaiming power from professionals who are sworn to secrecy and putting it in the hands and hearts of citizens who choose to disclose, discuss, imagine, and act. All by the simple act of sharing our unrecognized sorrows as well as our gifts.

◼ *Gift-Mindedness*

Citizens create satisfaction by recognizing their individual capacities and skills. We begin to see that the neighborhood is a treasure chest. By opening the chest and putting the gifts together in many different ways, we multiply the power of its riches.

A competent community builds on the gifts of its people. It knows that a gift is not a gift until it is given. Before it is given, it is only a beautifully wrapped box in a drawer. It is a capacity held in exile. Gifts need to be named and exchanged, not only to create a competent community, but also to create a functioning family. This is a family that has discovered its capacity to produce for itself, together with a competent community, all that is required for a truly good life, a satisfying life.

The tragedy of a dysfunctional family or neighborhood is that the potential gifts of its members are never given. The paradox is that in the midst of this, we can hold skills that are useful to systems but never find the satisfaction of turning our skills into the gifts that are so needed by our family or neighbor.

Gift-mindedness rests on the belief that satisfaction grows out of the understanding that what we have is enough. We already have most of what we need to create satisfaction in fulfilling the functions of raising a child, staying healthy, sustaining the land. The question becomes, "How do we combine what we have to create what these functions demand?"

We know that in communities, people have diverse values and visions. These differences in competent community space are valuable. The system world calls for alignment where differences are a problem to be solved. We also know that in communities that are not functioning well, differences are a great source of conflict.

When we decide to build a competent, functional community, we do not need to be divided by differences. In focusing on gifts, we get beneath them, or above them, to something more foundational where people can find common ground. We don't put people outside our value system; we include them in it. We speak to their gifts, rather than their differing values or vision.

I will speak to you as if you have gifts and are waiting to offer them. Beneath our differences are common concerns—for example, raising a child, concern for the land, being healthy. These are fundamentals that no one would argue with. A community that works is a place where you can fulfill these concerns and give your gifts.

Associational Life

Community competence and abundance are most likely to prevail in places where the consumer society and its institutions have not taken over. The consumer economy has invaded or colonized most every corner of life but one: associations and associational life.

An association is fundamentally a group of people who have a shared affinity. Associational life begins with a group of people who are drawn together for some reason, and that reason is what makes it work. Say they all like dogs, so they have a dog club. Or they all like reading fiction, so they have a book club. An association is often a fulfillment of one's individual likes and purposes. It is a place for having something in common, standing on common ground. But there is more to it than that.

Associations are a primary place in community where individual capacities get expressed. If I want to manifest my kindness or generosity, and I want to do it in a collective way, then I create or join an association. Association is a structural property of a competent community. It is the aspect of community that is repeatable; it has continuity and membership. Otherwise, it is a meeting. If you and I want to have breakfast together, good. If we want to ask two friends to join us and have breakfast every month, then we are an association. You can tell who is in an association. It has a boundary.

To choose to participate in associational life means you choose to be in a more formal relationship with a group of people. You want to be with them for your own interests. Few associations come together to do a social good. For people to do a real social good, they come together for some other reason and do a social good out of their peripheral vision. Otherwise, it is a system.

■ Individual vs. Communal Properties and Capacities

Gifts, association, and hospitality (properties) form the structure that allows people in community to manifest kindness, generosity, cooperation, forgiveness, and the acceptance of fallibility and mystery (capacities). We tend to think of all these capacities as individual traits. Here we want to think of them as communal traits. The point is that we can have satisfied individuals, but we can also seek satisfying communities.

For every property and capacity we have two possibilities. Let's use kindness as an example. One is individual kindness: She is being kind to you. The second possibility is that together we value kindness; therefore, kindness is called out from us in a way that may not be expressed by an individual. A hospitable community calls forth kindness from its members, and when this happens, something greater is produced. Here is the distinction: If I am kind, that is about an individual. I am a kind person and I am committed to kindness in the world. In community, I am part of a circle in which kindness is evoked and valued and named.

To deal with an individual property and a collective property, we can consider two ways that a property can be brought into the world. One is, "How do we do it together?" The other is, "How do we, together, allow me to do it individually?"

Suppose I say, "Let's you and me and her cook dinner for those people across the street who have lost a loved one." In this case, we are doing kindness together. We are collectively kind; we are performing an act of kindness as a group.

As for the second way, when I show kindness as an individual act in a competent community, I not only feel good but also am rewarded for being kind. This is a community that creates space for me to be kind and values it. It is a context in which kindness is welcome, appropriate, rewarded, and valued. In this context, kindness is nurtured. If, on the other hand, in the context of the consumer way, the meal is ordered and delivered from a restaurant, it is still a kind act. The problem is that while it is good for the economy, it does not build the social fabric of the neighborhood.

Families and neighborhoods become abundant and functional again when they invest enough in each other that gifts, association, and hospitality become commonplace in the collective. This invisible structure of community properties is created when citizens come together to produce something. It also is built when we come together out of sorrow, at a funeral, or out of joy, for a picnic or holiday.

■ *Kinds of Associations*

Associations come in three forms. First, associations can be defined by location. The Westwood Neighborhood Association. The South 10th Street Restaurant Owners Association.

Second, they define themselves by the functions they serve. For each of the functions of a community—educate a child, care for the vulnerable, protect the land, and the rest—there are associations. We have self-help groups, kindergarten parents' associations, green and open-space groups.

The third way we associate is by interest. Dog lovers. Marathon runners. Amateur gourmet cooks, book clubs, garden clubs.

You can almost see de Tocqueville chuckling at his description of what Americans will associate around; he said American associations are productive, prodigious, futile, and almost unimaginable at the same time. An example he would particularly enjoy is a group called Bikers Against Child Abuse. It is a national organization, with local chapters. They are leather-jacketed bikers—you can go to their website.

From Bikers Against Child Abuse, it's not hard to imagine what is hidden within the potential of associations and their manifestations around all kinds of issues. We would bet more on Bikers Against Child Abuse than on putting more child abuse workers in the neighborhood. Treating child abuse is not a commercial proposition for the bikers. The power of associational life is that money is taken off the table. It's all about "We do it," not "We buy it."

So, we come together because of where we are, who we are, and what we care about—we are interested in the same thing. Bikers Against Child Abuse is a good example of a group that is broadening its space. It moved from interest group to personal care.

■ Self-Organization

There is a paradox facing the competent community: Things have to be organized to get anything done, yet the most efficient ways to get things done are systems. The same systems that divert the vitality of community. Some form of organization is required. The traditional way of doing something is to have a system by which somebody manages things. The community way of doing it is to count on self-organization, which is very unpredictable and unmanageable. For the exchange of gifts to become the norm in a community, it needs to self-organize, with all its hazards.

A distinction we can make between managing and self-organizing is that self-organizing is creating some structure without someone being in charge. Managing is giving structure as the one in charge. It is the difference between convener and executive, between open space and system space. Associational life is essentially self-chosen order. Open space. System life is essentially imposed order. Closed and bounded space.

A self-organizing group is built and focused on people's gifts, whereas a managed system is built and focused on needs. For example, leadership in systems focuses on personal improvement goals based on what is missing. Leadership in community life goes to people for their gifts and focuses on what is present. This gift focus is how communities become competent. Attention will go to people's capacities. We can begin to say we are a healthful, educated, safe community because we have combined and organized our gifts. In this way, we become citizens once again, the producers of our lives.

This is the way a church supper happens at Countryside Methodist Church. Their process is different from that of someone who has expertise, such as a caterer or party planner. It is done by recognizing what each does well and getting them to do it. If you are going to build a house and you have a network of friends who have the skills you need, you get them each to do the thing that will get the house built.

How do we match what we have to do with who we are? The church supper is accomplished by what can be called a *gift-powered practice.* It is self-organized by offers and requests, not by assignment. When we focus on gifts, then the real question is how to inventory and assemble them. For the Countryside Methodist Church suppers, it happens informally. People say they would like to do a certain thing: Some bring bread, a condiment, something sweet. Some things may find no volunteers. And despite this, the dinner will take place.

■ ASSOCIATION OR SYSTEM?

We might ask, "When do associations become systems?" The answer falls along a continuum. And morphing from association to system is not necessarily an undesirable thing. We want some associations to become systems. We are not saying that systems are bad; they just don't satisfy many core human longings. For example, a lot of businesses start out associatively. In a way, Silicon Valley is an associational working place. "We met for months in our garage" is how Apple and a lot of others began. When invention and aliveness are needed, association is the form where they are most nourished.

The early stages of most systems began as associations. The example given by Alexis de Tocqueville, the French cultural observer who visited America in 1831, was the invention of American cities. Nobody had a plan. There were no urban planners. Until developers arose and systematized the process, people in association invented every one of our cities.

An association may become a system when the founders are replaced. There are exceptions, like Alcoholics Anonymous. The founders of AA are dead, and AA's members go on with a set of principles and the agreed-upon work to be done.

Many of our social services began as associations. A group of people get together in an association and they say we need a doctor, and they build a hospital to get the doctor to come. They create the institution.

■ *The Nature of Order in Community Space*

The system way is an ordering for the purpose of somebody other than the people producing it. The community way absolutely depends upon whatever is produced being what people want to produce. Community structure is based on desire; the system way is based on third-party interests and needs analysis.

Self-chosen order does have its challenges. People who hear about self-organization say, "But what if people don't want to do such and such?" The honest answer is that it will not get done. Then they say that someone has to do it, and they do it themselves. This is how an organic process works. No one claims that a community system is efficient. The question is, are we willing to live with some failure—that the banner did not get put up, the newsletter was three days late—in service of keeping people connected and accountable for fulfilling their own desires?

And what are we going to do anyway, fire people? Volunteerism was never designed to be efficient, only satisfying. Systems were never designed to be satisfying, only efficient. If productivity and low-cost results are our main purpose, the community way will frustrate us. You see it every day. There is a community meeting on an entrepreneurship project, and a person shows up an hour and ten minutes late. Very frustrating. The meeting was scheduled from one to two-thirty and Arthur comes in at two-twenty. What do you do? Talk about consequences and accountability? Lock the door? Of course what you say to him is, "Thanks for coming. Glad you made it. Have a seat. Can I get you a glass of water? Or a filet mignon? Better late than never."

That vignette goes to the heart of the matter. It is a purpose question. What are we there for? We are there to build community and connection. If we do not get much done until the final ten minutes, that may be the price of living in community. The purpose of community is community.

The key difference is between doing what we want to do and doing what someone else wants to do. In the world of community, after we figure out in the neighborhood everything we want to do, big blank spaces remain. Whereas, in the institutional world, what we mean by a niche is that there is this little space that has not been invaded yet, so let's go after it.

Over and over again, we find with institutional people that they cannot abide the idea that what is going to get done is what people want to do. And some things are not going to get done. So what? In the system

world, people go on vacation, people get sick. It is a measure of how fragile the systems are, that one little chink or unattended space will cause
so much unease.

This is not an argument against structure and order, just about how
they are produced. What we are talking about, in taking the path to community competence, is changing our relationship to order. Community
has a unique relationship to order. It creates the minimum that is needed.
In systems, the first thing we do is create more order.

What helps us to find common ground between system and community life is that we create order without predictability. This is what chaos
theory and emergent design are about. You can always create the structure
that takes you another step, and then you look around and see what you
have. This is emergent order. It is an argument against the blueprint. You
do not presume that order is predictable, because even a blueprint strategy
is not predictable. It just gives comfort and also has some use in naming
common ground and intent. It's like they say—in system life, what gets
implemented is Plan C.

■ A Matter of Choice

Since the core of association is choice, this is where the book club
gains its power. If I go to a neighbor's living room or the public library and
I see a bunch of people who have read a book and now are talking with
each other, the one thing that distinguishes the group from an institution
is that they want to be there and be together. Plus, no one is getting paid.

You cannot underestimate the importance of this threshold level of
connection. When people do something voluntarily, it is because they
care about it or it wouldn't stick. There is no cohesion without care; there
is no care without choosing freely to be there. They have not commercialized the relationship. There is an exchange but no commerce. This
is an economy of abundance, not scarcity. We could call this a citizen
ecosystem instead of a consumer ecosystem. The absence of barter is what
gives life to associational existence. In the book club, there is very little
management.

Book clubs probably go awry when someone tries to manage. When
you put a literature professor with a bunch of neighbors, you probably
have a problem. You see this in the efforts of publishers. They promote

the book club movement as a way of selling more books. They give you questions to ask, as if we could not talk about the book without them.

Almost everyone we know who belongs to a book club goes for the relatedness. When we ask, "What was the book you were talking about?" they have no trouble telling us. And then we ask, "What did you talk about in the book?" and there will be long silence. It is not about the book, it is about community.

■ COMMUNITY ORGANIZING

Another way of thinking about creating a competent and abundant community is to consider it a form of community organizing. Being connected in the way we are speaking of develops confidence that we can create change based on the gifts of all: the neighbor, the deviant, the care filled, the troubled, the elected official, and the formal leader.

This parallels how traditional community organizing developed common cause, which was by identifying a common enemy and relying on opposition to create a sense that we were in the same boat. Saul Alinsky, the father of community organizing, framed it as being bedfellows, having no permanent friends. This can be powerful and has a noble history; it is just not what we are talking about here. Plus, bringing people together against an outsider is the opposite of hospitality.

Community competence based on abundance is about bringing people together around possibility, not disappointment. This is in line with combining our gifts and valuing association. What we are giving voice to in our discussion is a more relationship-based organizing.

■ *Hospitality*

Hospitality is the welcoming of strangers. This is a third major property that defines an abundant community: There is always a welcome at the edge, regardless of how bonded the members of a community might be. A neighborhood is not really a competent or abundant community if strangers are not welcome.

Hospitality is the essence of community competence. In Chicago, the Greek restaurants remain in neighborhoods where the Greeks originally settled. The Greeks have moved out, but the restaurants are still there. You go to a Greek restaurant, you walk up to the door, the door opens, and the owner comes out and says, "How are you? Come on in. Welcome." He asks your name, wants to know where you would like to sit. Calls the waiter over and says, "Bring him something to drink on the house." You know you've come to the right place.

Hospitality is the signature of not only an abundant community, but a confident one. The extent of hospitality becomes a measure of the belief that people have in their community. When you do not have confidence and you feel separate or threatened, you are unable to be hospitable. When you have a life in a connected and confident community, it is welcoming; hospitality is generated because people feel so good about themselves that they want others to share it and they want to share the joy of others.

A wounded community does not have this capacity. Hospitality generates from trust and produces trust. It is what is missing in the world of fear and scarcity. In a world of hollowness, hospitality is what is most needed yet is so rare. If I am afraid, I probably won't invite somebody over.

Welcoming strangers is not just an act of generosity; it is also a source of vitality and learning. Before the global village, we needed people from other lands so that we could hear their stories, listen to their music, eat their food, get a glimpse into ways of living other than our own. Without the presence of strangers, our culture stagnates and ultimately disappears. We need to know them up close, with all our senses in play. Virtual substitutes, electronic connections to the strangers, are the consolation prize.

■ Friendship and Trust

One dynamic of the community we are describing is that it builds friendships. Friendship is dependent on combining enough gifts among a group of people that the properties of association and hospitality can be manifested. Out of this, kindness, generosity, cooperation, and other community capacities emerge.

The idea of trust is almost interchangeable with friendship. A community forms when people have enough trust that they can combine their properties and capacities into gifts. Friendship and trust are the means through which something that was an individual quality now becomes a communal reality. This is the loom on which these threads of community can be woven.

The conversation about trust exists in both system life and associational life. In a system it is expressed contractually, and in community it is expressed relationally. The distinction is its form, not its nature. In the competent community, we do not have to commercialize the contract. Trust, in association, is the difference between a contract and our word.

In the system world, trust also is a code word for loyalty—the constant wish of leaders is to be surrounded by people they can trust. Trust in this sense means that people will remain loyal. It also means that they are predictable, they will take my side. I trust them to do whatever is necessary in my interests. That kind of trust means they are manifestations of me. I trust that they will act in my stead.

Every theorist of civil society and social capital says the center of it is trust.

What does trust mean in the community world? Think in terms of the absence or existence of an explicit contractual relationship. In associational life, trust replaces the contract or pay that is the glue for holding systems together.

John's grandfather used to say that his word was as good as his note, and if you wanted a written contract, he was the wrong man. He was a significant businessman in upper Ohio, and he would not sign a contract. That meant everything to him. The integrity of his person was the certification of the deal. He chose trust as his currency.

■ Gift-Powered Practice

Because associations are voluntary and gift focused, they are a vehicle through which people develop trust in each other. This is the foundation for hospitality, and the place where cooperation, generosity, and other family and neighborhood capacities can begin to arise. If we are in search of these properties and capacities, we know where to find them; associations are organized to allow people to express just these capacities. Take, for example, the Logan Square Artists League, which is an association of neighborhood artists to support creativity. That is what an association is: a vehicle for sharing diverse gifts.

Whereas associations are organized to express the properties and capacities of a competent community, systems are organized to produce services and products. This distinction has particular meaning when it comes to relationships. Systems *use* relationships to produce products and services. Associations create relationships for their own sake. This has the effect of bringing forth the properties of kindness, generosity, and the rest.

Developing community properties and capacities is the secondary purpose of association. Associations exist to be a collecting place for them. They will allow these qualities to be brought into the collective. This is why we need associational life; otherwise, these capacities will remain hidden within ourselves, a gift ungiven. Association is built on people who are manifesting generosity, cooperation, and forgiveness. It provides a vehicle for the manifestation of that which is hidden in systems.

Community competence arises in the absence of the control-oriented relationship that is the hallmark of system life. Community life is structured around requests, not commands. As mentioned earlier, many in the leadership field have been trying for decades to get systems to shift from command and control to participative leadership. Making this point in systems is essentially going against their nature. Participative leadership aligns with the nature of community.

Community life creates order and structure in its own way. It is an order based on reciprocity. *You do the dinner, I will do the invitations.* Decisions are based on people doing the choosing, not being chosen. And based on gifts. The fancy phraseology is that community life is an *organic process,* one that arises from what is needed now, not one that is produced from the existing structure.

▦ *The Invisible Structures of Community*

Another way of thinking about all this is to look at the invisible structures of an abundant community. They are a set of rules and customs that are threads of community fabric, often called *social fabric.*

Think of an after-hours jazz club, where musicians gather because they want to play their music together. Half of them don't know each other. Four of them sit down together on the stage. You see them talk a little; one of them goes one, two, three, four; and they start playing something. It sounds wonderful, and even though they may not have ever seen each other before and have spoken only a few words, wonderful music emerges. To an outsider it is magical.

What is operating is a clear structure, but if you are not part of the jazz culture, the rules and customs that make the music possible are invisible. Similarly, the properties of gifts, association, and hospitality are the hidden structure of community life.

What is happening with the jazz musicians is that they know and agree very quickly to the rules. The rules are, first, to pick a melody. Someone says, "Let's play 'How High the Moon.'" Then someone says, "In F." The key. Someone else says, "One, two, three, four," setting the beat. That is all they need. The melody, the key, the beat. In the shortest of shorthands, the hidden order is exposed. But if you do not understand it, it is like magic.

On the other hand, a symphony orchestra is like an institution. It is the system way of creating music. How does it work? All of the musicians have sheet music with notes that tell them what to play. The conductor in front has a baton and leads them in playing it. It is a system way of manifesting music. It of course can be beautiful.

The jazz way is the community way of playing. The invisible structures of gifts, association, and hospitality create the possibility and are the rules of a competent community. They are always available and essential. Hopefully, by making them explicit, more of us can participate in producing magic.

Our key point is that as the consumer society has grown along with system life, associational space where citizens come together to exchange their gifts and welcome strangers into the circle has become less common. The symphony takes the place of the jazz band.

5 ▦ *Community Abundance in Action*

THE CONNECTIONS AMONG local people are what awaken the power of families and neighborhoods to weave the social fabric of an abundant and competent community. We have characterized these communities as having three major properties:

- **Gifts**, the raw material for community

- **Associations**, the process through which the gifts are exchanged

- **Hospitality**, what widens our inventory of gifts

Each property feeds the other two. When we focus on gifts, we can create association; when we have strong association, we can offer hospitality. But it can also be said that association builds gifts, and that hospitality invites association. The point is, one doesn't necessarily come before the other. Enter anywhere you like—the constraints of the printed page create the sequence of discussion here.

▦ *The Capacities of an Abundant Community*

Gifts, association, and hospitality create the conditions or rules for what we call the *capacities of a competent community*. Capacities reside in individuals and can be nurtured to exist in the collective. They are the core elements that need to be visible and manifest to create an abundant community, and a family and neighborhood that function.

The capacities of an abundant community are kindness, generosity, cooperation, forgiveness, and the acceptance of fallibility and mystery. All come from within and are part of our nature. They are outside the market.

An abundant community is one that values our capacities and assumes that they already reside within us. It has nothing in mind for us, nor does it treat us, or fix us. It takes what emerges and lets that become an asset for all of us. It lets you be . . . together.

At the same time, an abundant community opens the space for capacities like generosity and cooperation. We are worth something because we can contribute. What we contribute makes our community grow. It makes us real and whole. We want to give. The most satisfying thing is not buying, but giving. Self-expression is the greatest satisfaction there is. Giving our gift is the essence of satisfaction.

In the absence of opportunities to manifest the capacities of a competent community, we are led to seek them in the marketplace. Consumerism takes some of its vitality from people who are not gaining satisfaction in bringing their gifts into their family or neighborhood. The cost of seeking satisfaction in the marketplace is that any human quality that operates within it gets commodified or diminished at the moment of payment. Love is not for sale.

What follows is a brief description of the capacities that make a community competent.

■ Kindness

Kindness is a relationship to another that has embedded in it love, care, and respect. It is being conscious of the vulnerability and softness of another. It is the opposite of envy. Nietzsche argued that kindness and love are the most curative herbs and agents in human intercourse. Kindness is what you do if you want to have a group of people in community. Here, we could all learn from developmentally disabled people, who often have a sense of kindness that is not there among those of us who are strangely labeled "able."

Abraham Lincoln is a role model for a person in the system world who was noted for his kindness and his magnanimity, which is kindness from a position of power. Even absent position or power, kindness is high-minded, in the sense that it either accepts or overlooks the frailties of the human condition.

So how do you create authentic kindness in the world? The Highlander Research and Education Center in New Market, Tennessee, has a partial answer: They think that song and dance create kindness in the world. They think that telling your story creates kindness in the world. Those are the building blocks for Highlander: dance, music, storytelling.

■ *Generosity*

Generosity goes beyond kindness. It is the alternative to the world of barter. Generosity is to make an offer for its own sake, not its exchange value. Generosity comes from the Latin *generosus,* which means "of noble birth." It conveys a sense of the bountiful, lavish, copious, and abundant. Generosity clearly has its roots outside the market, not explained by barter or one-to-one exchange.

As we have stated too many times, systems and the marketplace are based on a context of scarcity. Generosity emerges from the ground of abundance. Systems treat generosity as naïve. The system or consumer world counterfeits generosity by offering something as a bargain, a sale, a good deal, a loss leader. It is like the cartoon of a father standing outside his store that has a large "going out of business" sign, saying to his child, "Someday, my child, this business will be yours."

In the system world of philanthropy, generosity is sometimes called "charity," which is really an unstable and false generosity because it is oriented around the needs and deficiencies of just one party in the transaction. Charity is demeaning in this way. As if you need me, and you have nothing but gratitude to offer in return. Charity says, "You have not earned this; I am giving it to you because you have so few gifts."

A context of scarcity makes generosity an artificial act. It can be called currying favor. You go to an elder in a culture of generosity, and it is considered respectful. You go to a supervisor in business, and they think you must want something. Generosity is viewed in a context of scarcity as self-serving. Here we consider it community-serving. Community competence depends on generosity. It creates a context for generosity.

■ *Cooperation*

When we put people in competition with each other,
for one to win, the other must lose.
—Alfie Kohn (paraphrased)

Alfie Kohn has written with great insight and passion about the limits and mythology we hold about competition. To riff on his simple definition, perhaps the definition of cooperation is: "For me to win, you must win." Or if winning is not the point, then: "For me to prosper and find satisfaction and have peace of mind, then you must prosper and have peace of mind."

Competition is a core value of the scarcity world of systems and the consumer economy. But it is more than just an economic structure. It takes the marketplace mentality and diffuses it into the whole of our lives. This proposition is so internalized that it is hard to imagine an alternative. It is said to be the only way to produce efficiency, effectiveness, high performance, and productivity. It is the illusory basis of the good life.

The consumer culture shortchanges the idea of cooperation. The system world puts prosperity and peace of mind in a competitive situation. We compete to raise our standard of living. We put our children in scholastic and athletic competition as a measure of their value. We believe that we have to beat somebody to win, and that is the point, the purpose.

Competition is a celebration of scarcity, which makes it about privilege. It differentiates us and is the basis of class division. We believe it is better to be on the top, dominating. This is justified as being inherent in "human nature."

The cost of competition is that you begin to take your identity from winning. There is a hollowness in an obsession with winning. This obsession is why sports are so pervasive as a metaphor in business. Cooperative or aesthetic pursuits would not justify the sacrifice we make for the system world. So much for art and nature.

The fallacy of competition is that when you win, you are forever a winner. Not so. The thrill of victory is measured in minutes, yet in the system world, winning is romanticized to be a durable and sustaining solution. The reality is that it is never enough. Competition rationalizes our dissatisfaction. It keeps us wanting more. What better way to fuel the consumer economy?

Cooperation is based on the belief that there is enough for each of us. In politics, it is called statesmanship. Cooperation, as statesmanship is in politics, is a commitment to work something out. It is concerned about the process we choose to handle an uncertain future. It is a willingness to debate and argue in a way that sustains the relationship, above all. Adams, Jefferson, Hamilton couldn't have disagreed more, but they were joined in the intimacy of caring for the whole, over and above having their way.

Caring for the whole may typically be thought of more as a feminine gift or capacity. Just notice the difference in how men and women enact competition and cooperation. You can almost literally see women's joy about cooperation. You can see men's joy about competition. Shifting the context of community from competition to cooperation brings the feminine more powerfully into play.

An example: There was a group of twenty women community organizers meeting for a day, and they were asked at the beginning what power meant to them.

We started going around the room, asking, "What is powerful to you?" The first one said something that all agreed with: "A potluck." There is not a man in the world who would say that. Potluck is the perfect example of gift giving, community building, hospitality, generosity, all of that in one little word.

■ Forgiveness

Forgiveness is the willingness to come to terms with having been wounded. Not an easy thing to do. In traditional community lore, the unwillingness to forgive was called a feud. The Hatfields and McCoys. Much of the collective violence in the world has a long history of injuries, often going back generations. In some ways, you could say that blaming a common other for what they have done to us is a bonding process. Maybe it builds community.

This is why we have been careful to make hospitality, the welcoming of strangers, a key property of community. One of the miracles of the late twentieth century was that South Africa created a process of collective and communal forgiveness, the Truth and Reconciliation Commission. If offenders stepped forward and confessed to their own violence and asked for forgiveness, and if it was given, they would not be subject to retribution for their crime. This was and is controversial, but it is significant that a process like this would become part of a national strategy to move a very wounded culture into a positive future.

Hannah Arendt, a philosopher who tried to comprehend the meaning of the Holocaust, stated that forgiveness is the key to action and freedom. She and South Africa and all of us, in a way, know that the act of forgiveness signals beginning again, anew. It is a form of redemption. That is why it is rare.

It is especially rare in a mobile society, where we are always moving on. In community, we cannot run from our history together. Forgiveness is required when we have to live together. Forgiveness means we find a way to accept fallibility in the world. We find a way to accept the dark side of our own past and somehow complete it. Not forget or pretend it did not happen, but discover that our unwillingness to forgive keeps us imprisoned and unable to either offer our gifts or receive the gifts of those around us who are most problematic. This is easy to say and hard to choose, but we do know that it is a community based on abundance that creates a context where forgiveness is more likely to occur.

■ Fallibility

A conspicuous capacity of abundant communities is their tolerance, their acceptance of human limitations. In community space, people's limitations are intertwined with their gifts. When a neurotic person comes into the room, they create space for all others who are neurotic or anxious or angry. In the system space, there is no room for what is wrong with us—except in the privacy of the annual performance review. It is secret, it goes in your file, you sign off on it, and it affects your pay. Other than that, it's "Keep your sunny side up."

Community is about accepting people's fallibility. It requires the willingness to live with people's imperfections, as stated earlier, more so than being willing to live with their transgressions, which call for forgiveness, or not. Human shortcomings have more of an afterlife than their sins.

Fallibility is a part of the human condition, and therefore a reality of the relational world. This is a key distinction we make here. Institutions are not good at surcease and sorrow, the whole tragic and sad part of life. They do not know what to do, because institutions are designed to last forever. They act as if they are immortal, which they are not. So failure, sorrow, and frailty threaten their mythology of eternal life.

Communities recognize and accept fallibility, and do not try to change it. So we will pray for you, we will do rituals. We have cultural ways of dealing with fallibilities and tragedies. The system way is to try to fix it; the community way is to memorialize it.

This relates to the earlier distinction between a condition and a problem. As soon as we call something a problem, it begs for a solution and we start shopping. When we view fallibility as a condition of being human, we see it is within the capacity of the family and neighborhood to deal with the condition and even see the gift in it.

This is the gift to us of the developmentally disabled. Their condition is a fact of life; it does not diminish them. Nor do our frailties diminish us. Our frailties are not who we are. In fact, they show that we are whole. That we are human. We can be whole in community life, but in systems we can only be half. The other half is the stuff we leave off of our résumé.

To elaborate on this, a distinction has evolved in the social service world between how to approach people who are developmentally disabled and how to approach people who are mentally ill. Our society has tended to be more supportive of the developmentally disabled than of the mentally ill. This is because everybody believes that a developmentally disabled person's disability is something they can do nothing about. A mentally ill person, on the other hand, is still viewed within a medical model. It is a disease. It is curable. If only we had the right drugs, if only she would take her meds, the challenge would disappear. Systems still dominate the world of the mentally ill. The developmentally disabled world is moving away from systems back into community.

An example of how abundant communities can show acceptance of human fallibility comes from Vancouver, British Columbia. The mayor advocated for and ran on a platform of dealing with the city's drug problem by using a policy of "harm reduction" rather than correction or cure. Imagine that. He won.

The premise was that drug users are people who are half full and half empty. The half-empty part we call *addiction*. We have tried to deal with the half-emptiness in two ways. The first is to correct them—put them in jail. The other way is to cure them; we put them in treatment centers. The research shows that neither approach works very well. But because of our judgment about addiction, drug users become criminalized or medicalized. Both strategies are expensive and have produced large industries of professional services and buildings to house them. None of it has achieved much success in reducing addiction, reducing trouble in the community, or improving the lives of the addicts.

The mayor advocated a third way, harm reduction. His essential message was, "Most people who are drug addicts are going to die of it, no matter what we do. If we want to do something about them, we can do more of what doesn't work—cure or correct—and it still won't work. Or we can take them where they are and ask, how can we get them in a life that will damage us the least, and them the least?"

There now exists the East Vancouver Association of Drug Users. It is a community development group. These people, who became free of being cured or corrected, say, "Our lives had been surrounded by people who always saw us as empty. Now we can actually contribute something."

The woman who was the chair of the group, after hearing how impressed we were by what she was working on, said, "Now don't get romantic about this. Every person in that room is going to die of drugs. And we are all going to die a lot quicker than you are. But the one thing this harm reduction does is not harm reduction. It allows us, for the rest of our lives, to contribute something. That is what you see. Our hidden gifts revealed."

How better to spend your final days than to be free to give your gifts?

■ Mystery

A competent community creates space for what is unknowable about life. This is another major distinction from systems. The acknowledgment of mystery has advantages: the sense of strength that comes from letting questions go unanswered, the sense of aliveness that comes from realizing there is more than what you know. All learning comes from moments of mystery.

Mystery is the answer to the unknown. In actualizing its abundance, a community welcomes mystery, for that is a catalyst for creativity. Mystery gives us freedom from the burden of answers. Answers are just a restatement of the past.

In system life, living with mystery is considered poor planning. Systems are organized around the desire for certainty, science, and measurability. Planning, goals, blueprints are a defense against mystery. Institutions are about eliminating mystery. They are concerned with risk reduction or risk management. Taking uncertainty out of the future.

One reason the consumer life is so seductive is this promise of safety. We submit to the consumer culture for the illusion of safety. It is a purchased answer to anxiety. A counterfeit offer to calm our nerves. The price we pay for this is our aliveness. We lose our willingness to accept the uncertainty of life, the mystery that is part and parcel of the human condition and a major competence of community.

Mystery is to the unknown as grief is to sorrow. What do you do when you do not know what is going to happen to you? You name it a mystery. It lets you go. It is a name for things we cannot fully know or control. John was a friend of Ivan Illich, a renowned social critic and philosopher. When they met, John would have a list of questions. He would look at his list and ask Illich a question. Often, Illich would look up at the birds and say, "It's a mystery." And that was fine.

The reason we need art in all its forms is to grasp the mystery in our lives, to recognize the mysteries around us. To get away from the preordained structured way of seeing things. That is why you can listen to a song over and over. You know exactly what is coming, and it still holds an element of wonder. Which may be the primary function of art and why it is so essential to sustaining community.

▦ The Culture of Abundance

Community culture holds the consumer economy at bay.
—David Schwartz

The word commonly used to denote community is *culture*. It is the embedded way that a group of people has learned how to live in a place. All of that learning is embodied in the community. A culture carries the messages and rules without having laws and media. We can see culture only when we step outside of it. That is why travel is broadening. It gets you into another culture and you can see your own. You don't really see your own until you see another one.

Culture means that here in this place, we do things in a particular way. We hold this above money. We have a particular way in which we survive and flourish. We eat in a certain way, live in a certain way, create in a certain way. We have art that is our own. We face illness, suffering, and death in our own way.

In the consumer society, we have homogenized and diluted our communal culture and replaced it with a market-defined culture. We have a culture of consumerism. This consumer culture dis-embeds from our culture the functions that traditionally worked to provide satisfaction and puts them in a marketplace. When you break a culture apart and say, "How can we sell kindness or care or cooperation? How can we sell it, train it, curricularize it?" you are dis-embedding from communities the properties that made them whole. This process is most evident in our efforts to export our culture to the global market.

In a communal culture, everything is personal, neighbors know me by name, I am valued, I have gifts to offer the community. There is opportunity for gifts to be given. There is an order to how we organize our world, but it is not rigid. There are creativity, spontaneity. There is tragedy, and we mourn and move on together and know that we have found our way. Families and neighborhoods have reclaimed their functions in achieving the aspirations we share for our children, our health and security, our environment and economic enterprises.

Three other cultural traits of an abundant community are worth noting: the way it treats time, allows for silence, and values storytelling.

Time

A hallmark of modernism is that time is something we seem never to have enough of. Perhaps the most important marker of an abundant community is to treat time as if we have plenty. Not so in systems. In systems, we "spend" time as a scarce resource. In systems, speed is an inherent value. The system views time as a problem. It is urgent about pace and blind to a view longer than tomorrow. In systems, speed is god and time is the devil. Speed is a core selling proposition for the consumer culture. Consumers will pay a premium to not have to wait.

Time is a condition in community life and a problem in systems. One of the signs that family and neighborhood life has been colonized by the consumer mentality is that we have given away leisure. The consumer marketplace now sells as a benefit the idea that you can do business in your home. Once upon a time, the argument for automating home life was leisure; now it is about productivity. Busy-ness—a more accurate way to spell *business*. Let's get down to busyness. The dining room is an office; the bed is a desk. So much for the sacred space of eating and sleeping, or whatever else a bed was once used for.

To be not in a hurry is a quality of community life. In systems, when we are interrupted, we say, "I'll get back to you." In community, if asked whether we are busy, the answer is, "Come on in." Our being together is the priority, the point.

The opposite of speed is slow, or a natural pace. It is intimately related to the idea of association and hospitality. In community, I am in control of time. I am biding my time. When I am in the institutional world, time controls me. I am on a schedule.

Time is not only about speed or pace; it is about who sets it. In community life, I possess time. In system life, time must be stolen. The truth is that many workers do exercise control over their time in institutions. People do it all the time. They call it *goldbricking*. Time in institutions makes us nervous. In community it is a gift.

Time is also a state of mind. When we choose the time, time disappears rather than passes. "How long does it take?" is a subjective measure. In a dentist's chair, ten minutes is a lifetime. When you are in love, or seeing a great movie, or lost in a great book, an hour is ten minutes. You don't want it to end.

For the family to reclaim its function and the neighborhood to awaken its power, we need to shift our relationship to time. One function of the family is to produce time for itself. Time together in the family has been disappearing. Fast food replaces the family meal. When there is a dinner hour, it is more like a meeting. We use it to schedule all the functions that we have outsourced. If there are children, sports and afternoon scheduling are the agenda; for younger kids, it is play dates. The function of being together and being present is gone. The skill in enjoying this time is disappearing.

Time is also necessary to appreciate "labeled" people. When we are with people who think, communicate, move differently than we do, we walk slowly, listen more carefully, speak more simply and clearly. Slowing down time is a critical factor in determining whether we can fulfill our community responsibilities. To have time, we must begin by stopping . . . then we can see who we are and what is possible.

Time, then, is an instrument that allows communities to become competent. A willingness to take time. Just think about the expression *taking time*. What does it mean "to take"? When I control time, I have taken it; it is under my control. I own my life when time is mine for the taking. When you "spend" time, it is a cost; we are consumers of time. Time in systems is scarce; in community it is abundant.

■ Silence

As with time, the consumer culture thinks silence is a problem to be solved. In the broadcasting world, silence is called *dead air*. A large segment of the electronics industry is designed to keep silence at bay, as if it were the enemy. We can now plug sound into our ears wherever we are. Walking, driving, sleeping, working. In the midst of our virtual life, we can choose our own background music to give inflection to our experience. We don't have to go to the movies; we have become one.

Our willingness to experience silence is a measure of the quality of how we are with others and becomes a measure of our connectedness to others, which is the essence of community. In a competent community, as in an intimate relationship, there is space for silence and it does not make us nervous. There is a quiet confidence in a group of people who can sit together in silence—the Quakers and Mennonites come to mind. Silence in this context takes on a spiritual dimension; it puts us in contact with the divine and our own growth. Silence is also a form of communion, and of intimacy. It is simply being with another, feeling the joy of our presence together.

If we want to create community, then we must make space for silence. Silence creates the opportunity for inwardness and reflection. It makes the space for thinking. It manifests the stance that thought has value. That thinking is an action step. In this sense, thinking is a form of doing.

Silence is also associated with listening. In silence, we are willing to listen to ourselves as well as others.

Communities become competent and find their abundance when they experience a quiet and sometimes silent satisfaction of being together. The acceptance of being over doing. Silence is a form of Being made visible beyond the veil of words. It is for many a practice, perhaps spiritual, that has a profound effect on how we connect with each other.

Finally, silence is associated with listening. In silence, we are able to listen to our children, our neighbors, and our opponents, people we consider to be strangers. In listening, we also open ourselves to the nature of our neighborhood. With silence, we can learn about the place where we live because we can hear and see the messages of the trees, the plants, animals, and the buildings around us. They are a part of our community with much to teach, once we listen.

■ Storytelling

A culture is built through the stories we tell and what we choose to talk about—our narrative. The stories of a competent community are a narrative about our talents, properties, and gifts. Every culture has its creation stories about the origin of the sun and its energy, the land and its natural capacity, the source of life and the divine power that watches over it. These stories are teaching images, most often about the nature of the world and our place in it. Stories about what is natural, not what is synthetic and manufactured. There is yet to be a creation myth about how plastic came into being.

A primary function of a family, neighborhood, or community is to create its story. Telling the story gives body to the collective. In church, it is called *witnessing*. Remember how we did this and how we did that?

Communities become competent when people tell stories that link to their gifts. You want to know our story? Let me tell about how six of us came together and built that shelter in the park. How we had one person who seemed to be so mean but relented in the face of our kindness, who softened when we got to know them. These stories are the beginning of myths that memorialize and keep us reminded of the epic nature of our journey together.

Youth will say that no matter how much trouble I get into in the world, I go home and they let me in. I have been in a lot of trouble, but when I go home, they accept me. Inviting stories is the single biggest community-building thing that we can do, especially when the stories we tell are stories of our capacities, what worked out. Since stories tell us what is important, speaking of our capacities establishes them as the foundation upon which we can build a future.

The stories about our gifts, about how our kindness, our generosity, our trust, our forgiveness define us and give our life meaning—this is where an authentic sense of identity comes from, not from what we buy. The community way occurs when we have a culture that makes naming what works well acceptable and easy.

▦ *The Citizen Economy*

[A modern economist] is used to measuring the "standard of living" by the amount of annual consumption, assuming all the time that a man who consumes more is "better off" than a man who consumes less. A Buddhist economist would consider this approach excessively irrational: since consumption is merely a means to human well-being, the aim should be to obtain the maximum of well-being with the minimum of consumption. . . . The less toil there is, the more time and strength is left for artistic creativity. Modern economics, on the other hand, considers consumption to be the sole end and purpose of all economic activity.

—E. F. Schumacher

The discussion of a competent community is not complete without some attention to the local economy. Our capacity to be prosperous is increased by the existence of supportive purchasing habits of a community. Every immigrant group survived initially by creating a circular flow of money that stayed within that community. We know that strong neighborhoods are ones with a functioning locally owned business district.

There is a corollary in economics that fits with the gift-mindedness and ethos of abundance that are essential for a competent community. In most conventional theories of economics is an assumption that for there to be value, there must be scarcity. That assumption is part of what keeps us addicted to consumption. It means we have to remake our economy into one that supports the citizen and makes the consumer a secondary consideration.

This is a big shift. The 2009 *New York Times* article mentioned in chapter 3 moans about how reduced consumer spending in Japan is hurting its economy.[19] People are wasting less, they're wearing clothes longer, only 25 percent of young Japanese men want a car, young Japanese women have cut back on their fashion buying—all what we are talking about here. What was once purchased now has to be home- and handmade. To the traditional economist, ending our addiction to consumption is a financial nightmare. This is why we need to reframe what we mean by prosperity.

Most communities have the inherent capacity to provide what they need—in other words, to be prosperous. Prosperity is the belief that we can make do, find a way, and provide for ourselves. Not all that we want, or all that is possible, but enough. Prosperity is associated with the decision that we can produce a handmade life.

Traditionally, people who grew up with no money did not label themselves poor. They believed they had a future, even though the present was difficult. Poverty, on the other hand, is not just the absence of money; it is also the absence of a belief in a future. A competent community increases the likelihood of a better future. What we need for real prosperity is what money can't buy. And when we do spend money, we do it with some consciousness about the impact of that dollar on our community. This is prosperity.

This prosperity comes from operating in a local economy. An economy based significantly on barter and local resources. We use our money and capacities to support the local community. Call it a citizen economy, one based on gifts and local abundance. Such an economy would recognize the importance of the local marketplace.

Developing a citizen economy requires a shift in how we think of economics and markets. Take a classic definition of *economics* in a 1932 essay by Lionel Robbins: "the science which studies human behaviour as a relationship between ends and *scarce* means which have alternative uses [italics ours]."[20]

The human cost of the consumer or scarcity model is the loss of local gifts and capacities—all we have been discussing throughout this book.

What is valued gets narrowed to what is scarce, or made scarce for the sake of the market and the wages and profit that are created.

The citizen economy is concerned with human behavior as a relationship between ends and *abundant*, not scarce, means. It puts power in the hands of the community to define what has value and does not try to control that abundance by marketing needs.

The citizen economy gives form to the belief that the local exchange of goods and services supports a community's competence. That my well-being is dependent on participating in a local marketplace, on being able to walk to the "point of purchase." This means that we create a communal context wherein we value local capacities, resources, and talents over and above what gets monetized. In other words, the citizen economy is a mixture of a gift exchange and currency economy where people believe that much of what we need we can find locally, which keeps the currency local. Many communities have institutionalized this with their own local currency. The Schumacher Society led the way in publishing the best theory and practice in this. *Yes!* magazine also is a great source of what is possible and working.

The underlying premise of this thinking about prosperity is that if the community becomes competent, we require less from the system world. We ask, "What are we purchasing and where are we getting it from? How can we better satisfy what we need from ourselves?" You don't know what you need until you know what you have. Then you know what you have to buy from the outside.

The power of this thinking about a local economy is that gifts and capacities are not subject to systems and their requirements. The resources of a neighborhood are not organized to manipulate or manage or input services packaged as benefits. They are not designed to create dissatisfaction. Gifts obtained locally only wait to be noticed and named: This is the remedy for all the dissatisfaction we experience in the consumerist culture. A competent community will value what is locally created and sold. It will value the goods and services of a neighbor over a seemingly cheaper version that is imported.

A community becomes competent when each person knows that their own success, personally and economically, is dependent on the success of their neighbors and that what their neighbors sell and exchange is enough. This is the shift from an economy of scarcity to one of abundance.

▦ *Policies That Support Abundant Community*

Much of this book is about the limitations of systems and ways to place more choice and control in the hands of citizens. Here we want to reflect on what system and institutional policy can accomplish to support the local community's ability to nurture its gifts, welcome strangers, and strengthen associational life.

One major reason for the deactivation of our neighborhoods is that institutions often take on as their own purpose what rightfully belongs in the hands of local citizens. Institutions adopt the language of community building, but too often, despite good intent, they encourage dependency and reduce the power of local communities. Institutions promise a life of safety, education, health care, all we have talked of earlier. When neighbors and citizens agree to this intrusion of function and power, the capacity of both parties is limited.

Neighborhoods lose in two ways. First, our institutions fail to deliver on their promise to keep us healthy, safe, and prosperous; and thereby all of us, institutions and citizens alike, become more skeptical and cynical, and keep calling for more control and accountability. We see this in our growing distrust of government, public schools, physicians, and institutional services of all shapes and sizes.

Second, citizens grow rusty from failing to do what only they themselves can do. Their community skills are weak from lack of use. They succumb to isolation and being "well serviced." They reduce their trust in their neighbors who live three dwellings away and farther. Their community vision is blurred from the dependency created by focusing on nothing but big systems.

So the question becomes, "What can systems and institutions do to help citizens recover the power of their families and neighborhoods?" What can systems do, other than trying harder and doing more of what they now do? Below are some ways that our major institutions can become more friendly to and supportive of neighborhood efforts.

■ *Community-Friendly Policies*

Two basic questions arise when analyzing policies: Which policies should be stopped or altered, and what new policies can be adopted?

For both of these questions, some simple principles can guide institutions toward community-friendly positions:

- Respect and enhance life on a *small scale*. For example, government can take the stance that neighborhoods are places too small to fail. We have seen how large systems are kept alive because they are too big to fail. We could adopt a policy of too small to fail. Or there could be an "endangered neighborhood" conservation movement. Right up there with saving the spotted owl, preserving historic buildings, and conserving national parks.

- Understand that people's *gifts* are more valuable than their deficiencies and needs. Social services could approach residents as though helping them to manifest their skills, gifts, and capacities were one of the primary functions of each agency.

- Recognize that the power of community grows out of ever-increasing *cooperative local relationships* and connections. Schools could teach and provide constant experience with cooperative activity rather than emphasizing competition in sports and individual performance in classrooms. All learning and performing comes from cooperation, including evolution.

- Understand that a *local place* called *neighborhood* has unique, irreplaceable value. Businesses could cease the thoughtless transfer of families from "anyplace to anyplace" so that the family has no place called home and no relationships with continuity and trust. Same with agencies relocating vulnerable people to "nicer" housing and locations.

- Recognize that *local resources* are vital to the well-being of a community. A local economy is essential. Local governments, schools, and parks could consistently purchase their goods and services from local merchants and entrepreneurs.

- Understand that the economy and community each derive their power from *maximizing opportunities* for all the local residents to use their skills and contribute all their gifts. Government funders and foundations could make their grants to local communities that include marginal residents as productive citizens in their proposals.

■ A Listening Table

Local families, neighbors, and neighborhood associations are the most important voices to describe those things institutions should stop doing. They are also the best voices to describe how institutions could create new policies that would support and enhance powerful neighborhoods.

Institutions can convene Listening Tables of neighbors and their representative associations to establish an agenda for community friendliness. Connectors in local neighborhoods can create their own groups to develop an agenda for institutions that want to become friendly. Either way, these initiatives can create a dialogue that begins to redefine the powers and responsibilities of institutions and communities.

This dialogue can be framed by three questions:

First: What functions can neighborhood people perform by themselves?

Second: What functions can neighbors achieve with some additional help from the institutions?

Finally: What functions must institutions perform on their own?

The order of these questions is very important. It shows that the basic productive force is the local community. What citizens can do for themselves is the primary question. What institutions can do is a secondary question. A neighborhood doesn't know what it needs from outside until it is clear on what is has inside.

A system that implemented this philosophy can be found in Savannah, Georgia. Henry Moore, who was assistant city manager, created an innovative city system for nurturing neighborhoods called Leading by Stepping Back.[21] He understood that institutions can "invade" communities with programs and professionals who displace the capacities of residents and their associations. His first principle was to step back. The second was to listen to residents. To listen directly and in person . . . to residents.

No surveys, no speaking to those who "speak" for residents. He talked to people in neighborhoods. He and his staff went directly to citizens to ask: What do local residents want to do? What tools do they have to create their vision with? And then, how can city government assist? The third part of the city's strategy was to provide small neighborhood grants to help people improve their block.

■ *A Neighborhood Impact Statement*

As the environmental movement grew, one of its goals was to effect government policy. Members of the movement wanted government to stop supporting policies that hurt the environment and to initiate policies that would help. One legislative result of the movement's efforts was the *environmental impact statement*. This law required government to carefully review the effect on the environment of any new construction or industry and to write a statement of its findings. Citizens could then review the statement and file their own comments on its validity. This process has had a major impact on public environmental policy because it makes issues and choices visible.

What is of special significance is that the law does not only try to protect the environment in general. It recognizes that many initiatives mainly effect the environment in a particular place in a particular way. The same is true of institutional initiatives affecting neighborhoods. They often affect different neighborhoods in different ways, and often these initiatives affect only one particular neighborhood.

A major policy change to set limits on systems and their local effects would be to require a *neighborhood impact statement*. The statement would ask the institution to outline the action it proposed and the impact it would have on the social fabric and local economy; this statement would go alongside existing impact studies on the environment, health, and safety of a neighborhood.

Local residents and associations would then be alerted to the institutional action and could do their own public assessment of the impact on their community life. Based on this process, a useful dialogue could develop regarding how an initiative might become a win–win scenario.

Any level of government, business, or nonprofits could adopt the neighborhood impact statement idea. As the unity and strength of communities grew, they could devise and lobby for neighborhood impact statements of their own design.

■ *Money Matters*

In many neighborhoods, the lack of a decent income is a major limiting force on the power of residents to perform their functions. The sustainable answer to this is to build a viable local economy.

The common institutional response to neighborhoods whose people don't have enough money for necessities is to provide them with social services. Often, the dollars appropriated for these services are so great that if the same dollars were allocated to supplement the incomes of low-income people, no resident would live in poverty.

This pattern first emerged in a U.S. study that showed, between 1960 and 1985, that federal and state cash assistance programs grew 105 percent, while non-cash programs for services and commodities grew 1,760 percent. By 1985, cash assistance programs amounted to $32.3 billion, while service and commodities programs received $99.7 billion.[22]

In 2008, the same pattern prevailed. The major family welfare program, Temporary Assistance for Needy Families (TANF), allocated 40 percent of its funding for cash and direct benefits meeting basic needs, while allocating 60 percent for services.[23] And because most of the professionals who provided the services did not live in the low-income neighborhoods, the service dollars were drained from the poor neighborhoods to support middle-class economies elsewhere. Many government employees are required to live locally in recognition of this concern.

What the studies suggest is that the basic public policy change could shift from service to income strategies. Also, income strategies should shift from cash toward incentives for local businesses to employ local people. If we had taken the billions for social services designed to "fix" poor people and used them for investments that ensured their participation in the economy, we would not need to "fix" poor people.

■ Gift-Minded Philanthropy and Funding

Many foundations, along with governments, fund social services to assist neighborhood people. Much of this funding is based on "needs surveys" that result in the intervention of outside experts and professionals in the neighborhood. An alternative policy would be for funders to establish guidelines that began by identifying the neighborhood's assets—the gifts of residents and their associations. Grants would be allocated to neighbors who planned to connect their assets in ways that created new relationships for improving health, safety, economy, and the lives of people.

This asset approach is outlined for funders in a document titled *Discovering Community Power*, which can be downloaded from the publications at the Asset-Based Community Development Institute's website.[24] It offers guidelines for policy that builds neighborhoods rather than investing in more service institutions.

◼ Keeping the Money in the Neighborhood

Governments maintain many local institutions: schools, parks, libraries, police stations, and more. Each of these institutions purchases goods and services in order to perform its functions. Usually, a central purchasing office uses taxpayer money to purchase these goods and services. And most often, it purchases them from large institutions, typically located in a distant place.

A neighborhood-friendly policy would be to give priority to buying from local businesses and local home-based entrepreneurs. One illuminating example occurred in an urban neighborhood where a local middle school principal thought her students would learn a great deal if they could be associated with local businesspeople.

Across the street from the school was a locksmith's shop. The school was frequently broken into, and a national locksmith company had the contract to repair locks for the entire school system. The principal persuaded the central purchasing office to allow her to contract lock repairs with the local locksmith. Then she asked the locksmith to let her students visit and see him at work. Soon, two students became intrigued by locksmithing and visited every day after school, informally apprenticing for the occupation. At some point, the locksmith began to pay them a small stipend.

The principal prepared an inventory of all the goods and services the school purchased. She had the list distributed to the local merchants and arranged to buy from them the products they could provide. In exchange, she asked them to introduce her students to their work and skills.

This local purchasing policy shift created prompt and personal school suppliers. It boosted the market of local businesses, recycled local taxpayers' money in the neighborhood, and opened vocational and economic opportunities for young people.

Critics might say that this local purchasing policy may not provide goods and services at the best price. Whether or not this is true depends on how you account for costs. On the surface, central purchasing may seem the low-cost alternative if you just measure purchasing dollars. You get a different cost picture if you look at all the costs of funding the central purchasing office, such as the cost of pollution created by long-distance transportation of goods, the cost of local young people feeling useless and jobless, the cost of a weak local job market. The policy issue is whether our accounting system is based on the best price or the best value. Systems create prices. Community building creates value.

■ *Neighborhood Jobs*

We know that local people employed by local businesses are a major neighborhood economic resource. They not only create payroll, but they reduce or eliminate transportation costs and often have more flexible, family-friendly working schedules.

Local chambers of commerce and neighborhood business groups already work hard to develop local business. What they most often do is focus on supportive financing and collective marketing. They rarely work on the local employment side. They could agree to post all job opportunities on the neighborhood website or in public places. They could initiate a local currency program partnering with neighborhood associations to help make it successful. Each of these is not so much about a specific program as it is about systems' becoming conscious of the need for a local bias.

■ *A Penny Saved Is a Penny Loaned*

Financial institutions have a well-publicized history of redlining, questionably ethical loan policies, excessive interest rates, and loose credit card policies that has had a major impact on neighborhoods.

Adopting a policy of deepening our commitment to local saving and lending groups typically called *credit unions* could reduce these abuses. Just as government has "bailed out" our larger financial institutions, it can "bail in" local credit unions that recycle neighborhood wealth so that a penny saved is a penny loaned. The public policies supporting a renewed neighborhood credit union movement would provide start-up grants, deposit insurance, technical assistance, and special financial incentives for neighbors who started and maintained a new account.

This policy would require a major reeducation effort to help citizens make better decisions about managing their money, choosing savings over consumption and being less seducible by the siren of upward mobility and the good life.

■ A Time for Every Season

If you ask people why they don't do more in their neighborhood or community, a common answer is that they just don't have time to connect their gifts and benefit from associational life. There is some truth in this. Instead of producing leisure, we are now consuming it. The consumer world persuades us to measure well-being by money, and so the bills arrive while we are buying more stuff at the mall. The remaining free time is used for driving kids to receive more services called lessons, workouts, team sports, and various forms of rehab.

Powering the family through a day in the consumer society is exhausting—and never really satisfying. This has produced the modern phenomenon called *quality time*. So neighbors say, "We don't have quality time for the kids, much less the neighbors and the neighborhood."

The policy implication of this draws our attention to the way our institutions eat up our working time and govern our slide into consumerhood, which drives us to use our time in shopping, transporting, and watching images on glass screens.

Of all the policy changes necessary to reactivate our community life and the care of our democratic society, redefining the uses of time is most important and most difficult. To make time available requires a radical shift in institutional policy and a cultural shift by neighbors who are accustomed to trying to buy a life rather than making a life.

The recognition of time as valuable for families has begun to occur in fits and starts. We mentioned earlier how W. K. Kellogg shortened the workweek to allow for more civic and family time for his company's employees. Some institutions have adopted *flextime* policies allowing employees to create their own work schedules. Other institutions have established family and pregnancy leave policies. However, these are merely beginnings and apply to a minority of workers.

A more comprehensive policy shift could be precipitated by governments, United Ways, or major civic associations by convening an Inter-Institutional Table. The Table could initiate a more comprehensive policy shift. It would provide a forum for creating community-friendly policies that focused first on opening up time for families and neighborhoods to perform their critical functions. From these discussions, the Table could proceed to define and implement other community-friendly policies, including those discussed earlier in this chapter.

■ *Moving from Here to There*

To conclude this discussion of policy shifts, we need to address the question of who will design and create new policy. Normally, when we convene experts to study problems and recommend policy, we pick a *blue ribbon* committee or task force. The blue ribbon is for first place, the winners. These winners are most often the incumbent leaders in the system world. Maybe a few outsiders are added for color. This means that those redesigning the system enter the room with the belief that more and better services will create better outcomes.

This is the disease deciding on the cure. At the core, this process most often has program experts taking another look at old deficiencies. They produce recommendations about what new funding is needed to fix old needs with more programs.

It is true that the work of every expert panel has a step called *citizen engagement*. This usually means the experts take "input" from citizens and formulate recommendations; then they position the recommendations so that citizens will "feel heard." "Getting input" is a form of lip service that keeps ownership and control in system hands.

What is required are reform groups who can suggest new thinking rather than more programs—groups who have the insight that the system that created their own particular task force is, by its nature, limited in its impact, regardless of what gets recommended.

The strategic challenge is whether we can value regular citizens, non-system people, and believe that they are competent to create new policy. Is it possible for non-system people to create policy along lines that are independent of the group that commissioned them?

If this is possible, then we need policy that grows from people and thinking that rejects the conventional beliefs about efficiency and accountability. These beliefs inevitably focus on measuring services by assessing their size, their growth, and the number of people served. As soon as you decide to measure the value of a "service" this way, you have taken off the table the major elements that can make the most difference: citizens and their ability to create community.

If policy is developed only by system experts looking at system services, then nothing will change. Local citizens looking at neighborhood gifts are the primary group that has the power to change lives, heal wounds, and produce healthy communities. In this way, the process of creating policy, in itself, begins to produce the kinds of effects that the policy itself is aimed at.

Regardless of the efforts at system change, ultimately each of us has to initiate the policy shift from the seat in which we find ourselves. A stunning example of this is Broadway United Methodist Church in Indianapolis, Indiana, where Mike Mather is pastor. He and the church decided that their service programs were not working. The programs were not changing the living conditions of the low-income neighborhood where the church is located.

They stopped the food programs, the education programs, and the youth programs. For the youth, they realized that neither correction nor cure was really helping. They decided that the problem of these kids is their isolation. Their lack of connection. Not knowing what they are good at. Or how good they are. So the church began to simply connect the youth to each other and to people in the neighborhood.

The church wants to do something about health and has decided that better health grows out of a strong social fabric. So, with the support of a local foundation, they are planning a program where money will be available for any group of three people from different families to do anything these people think will help the neighborhood. The strategy is to create small groups and keep the money in the hands of local people.

The church also has a strategy to support local enterprise. They know there is a lot of entrepreneurial spirit on every street corner. People are doing hair on front porches, selling meals from their kitchens, selling candy, doing sewing, fixing cars, caring for pets and children. As an institution, this church has decided to create an export economy in the neighborhood.

Broadway Methodist will help neighbors expand their businesses and maybe connect with others in nearby neighborhoods to see what they can initiate together. They know that when a bunch of businesses of the same kind are concentrated together, those businesses are more successful. Retail stores, restaurants, antiques. Food service here, cars there, produce grown in the neighborhood across the street. Then the neighborhood businesses can share resources, people, learning, looking out for each other to cut labor cost. The institution—in this case a church—becomes an organizing agent rather than a service-providing system. This is the essence of the policy shift that is emerging from neighborhood-minded systems.

■ *Democracy and the Abundant Community*

The purpose of a democracy is to provide the opportunity for citizens to create abundant communities.

Democracy is a structure and a process built on a belief in self-governance, freedom, and an engaged citizenry. In the United States, the founders cared most about our freedom and distinguished it from license. They made clear that there is a purpose for being free. That purpose is defined in the Bill of Rights, in the First Amendment to the Constitution—which grants freedom of expression and freedom of assembly among others.

The founders believed that these freedoms were not passive. They understood that if we failed to use these freedoms, democracy would wither away. This book is about the use of these freedoms so that democracy will flourish.

The community described in this book has at its center two sources of power: the expression of our gifts and their manifestation through association with our neighbors. These are the same powers that the founders understood as the purpose of our freedoms in a democracy. Without their use, democracy loses its purpose.

In 1958, the U.S. Supreme Court explicitly extended freedom of assembly to include freedom of association.[25] Not only the right to gather, but the right to join. A community without the relationships of association where our gifts can be expressed and magnified is a black hole at the center of democracy. It is a place where the essential freedom that creates democracy is abandoned. It is a place where people are housed in isolation. They are not interdependent citizens. Instead, they are isolated consumers, sadly, unknowingly contributing to the decline of our democracy.

Freedom of speech not only is about expressing our opinions, but also can be seen to be about our freedom to declare and give our gifts. We care so much about freedom of expression because it resides at the essence of our humanity; it is in our nature to need to give our gift, to have our uniqueness manifested. And government and systems threaten that space.

We affirm how precious our gifts are when we create prisons. Prison is a societal decision to take away your freedom and thereby is a place where we say you are not free to give your gifts. Taking away your capacity to give your gifts is the worst thing we can do to somebody. The opposite of freedom is that you cannot give your gifts. In prison, we will keep you alive—we will feed you, give you shelter and health care—but we will not allow you to give your gifts. There is one other point to be made about the founders' focus on expression of gifts and relationships of association. They understood that creating a new society is a tremendous, challenging, demanding undertaking. The democracy needed great power to meet this challenge.

For more than a century, we have seen an attempt to claim that power comes from competition and the marketplace. As if commerce itself is what ensures our freedom. The idea of freedom has become aligned with the marketplace, the free market.

This is a recent construction, however. There was no mention of competition or the marketplace in the founding documents. Perhaps they understood that an economics that serves us well is *not* about the allocation of scarce resources. A scarcity mentality that justifies competition has nothing to do with sustaining our freedom.

A scarcity mindset and its consequence, competition, develop political effects. We become willing to give up more and more autonomy. We remain ignorant of knowing what inherent and natural gifts surround us. We lose touch with our neighbors and do not assemble or associate. All the things we so believe in are not taken from us; we give them away freely.

Extending the book's point of view, we might say that a community based on scarcity, dependent on systems, with citizens competing and living in isolation from one another, threatens democracy. That is why consumerism threatens democracy. Because it is organized around scarcity and dependency by design. This scarcity and dependence are inherent in a consumer economy and do not serve democracy well.

On the other hand, the founders took the position that the power for a new democratic society needed to be abundant, based on cooperation and available to everyone. So they focused on protecting the abundant sources of power: the expression of personal gifts and the means to express them—unbounded associations.

The abundant community is therefore the purpose of democracy. It allows us to be citizens once again, knowing that we have the power to define our own possibilities, decide what choices reside in our own hands, and choose our own future. We no longer require great leaders—not even a strong, "developed" economy—only each other, in association, coming together with our gifts in mind. We are, however, required to join an association, share our gifts, and become the principal producers of our future.

PART III

Creating
Abundance

HOSPITALITY *is not to change people, but to offer them space where change can take place.*

It is not to bring men and women over to our side, but to offer freedom not disturbed by dividing lines.

It is not to lead our neighbor into a corner where there are no alternatives left, but to open a wide spectrum of options for choice and commitment.

It is not an educated intimidation of good books, good stories, and good works, but the liberation of fearful hearts so that the words can find roots and bear ample fruit.

It is not a method of making our God and our way into the criteria of happiness, but the opening of an opportunity for others to find their God and their way.

The paradox of hospitality is that it wants to create emptiness—not a fearful emptiness, but a friendly emptiness where strangers can enter and discover themselves as created free; free to sing their own songs, speak their own languages, dance their own dances; free also to leave and follow their own vocations.

—Henri Nouwen

6 ▓ *Awakening the Power of Families and Neighborhoods*

THIS BOOK IS AN INVITATION to participate in a transformation and movement that is occurring in many modern and developing societies. That movement is the search for an alternative, more community-based way to live and find satisfaction even when surrounded or assaulted by a consumer culture.

▓ *Competence within Reach*

The starting point in every transformation is to think differently. We have used the shorthand of contrasting the system way with the community way in order to characterize the shift. It is a movement from purchasing what turns out to be dissatisfaction, to producing satisfaction. To shifting from the lens of consumption to the lens of citizen community as the core resource for a satisfied life.

▪ *We Are Enough*

Making the shift requires only that we act as if each of us and all of us have all that is needed to break our habits of consumption and its limits to satisfaction. We have the gifts, the structures, and the capacities needed right now. We have the capacities in our families and in our communities. All we need to do is shift our thinking first and then act on that shift. This is true, independent of the culture we live in, east or west, urban or rural, rich or poor.

When we stop looking to the marketplace for what matters to us, we find ways that neighborhood and community can provide much of what we require. This is the place to begin the discussion about what we all can do.

In the realm of doing, there is a community world around us that is now doing much of what is needed; it is simply invisible. Our modern media is just not that interested. The overpowering spotlight of the consumer world and the system world shines so brightly that the community world lives in its shadow. We want to magnify that neighborhood and community world to make its blessings more accessible and usable. We want to magnify the power of connectedness as the antidote to the symptoms and dis-ease of consumerism.

■ What We Seek Exists Around Us

To some extent, each of us already participates in the neighborhood and community world. We belong to some organizations and know that more associations exist around us. We have our network of friends and neighbors. Each of us has a set of gifts that when named, collected, and offered can provide great satisfaction. We are already on the path to becoming more powerful citizens and avoiding many of the costs associated with being consumers.

What is needed is for us to more fully engage as citizens and to shift our attention, our narrative, toward the community way that we can reclaim. Community properties and family capacities can become the centerpiece in fulfilling our desire for a satisfied life.

In chapter 4, we defined community competence in terms of nurturing the existence of three properties: gifts, association, and hospitality. Community competence is the capacity to make gifts widely available, to make association life thrive, and to welcome strangers into the center. These can be accomplished locally, and we want to outline how both simple and profound this can be.

We begin with a perspective on the culture of community.

■ *Building the Community Culture*

Every community creates its own culture—the way the community members learn, through time, how to survive and prosper in a particular place. Displaced people lose their culture. But it is also possible to lose a community culture even though you stay in a place. Many of us have lost our culture, even though we live in a neighborhood, occupy an apartment, see others from a distance.

The question is how to create another way of life, so that we could say, "In this place, we have a strong culture where kin, friends, and neighbors surround us. We are a group of families who have a special kind of relationship. Together we raise our children, manage health, feel productive, and care for those on the margin."

The culture of community is initiated by people who value each other's gifts and are seriously related to each other. It takes time, because serious relationships are based upon trust, and trust grows from the experience of being together in ways that make a difference in our lives.

■ *Lessons from the Pioneers*

If we need a community that will make a difference in our lives, and we can't buy it or create it through a program, where do we start? It is a great puzzle. While we are not suggesting that we return to an earlier time, the early history of the United States and Canada gives us a clear direction to pursue.

The first European pioneers who settled down in a new place had a daunting task. Perhaps they were two families with children. They arrived in the wilderness with two covered wagons and a few oxen to pull them. Inside the wagons were simple tools, a trunk or two, and basic provisions. They were at the beginning of creating a new community. Perhaps if we understood how they did it, we could see how we could do it, too.

What did they have? There was some land, their tools, and themselves. These were the assets they had with which to create a homestead and, shortly thereafter, a hometown. It would all have to be home produced and often handmade. And because of that, everything they created was an expression of themselves—their vision, their knowledge, their skills, and their limitations. The result was a community in which they had pride, because they had created it.

This new community was the creation of families: Mary, Sam, and their children; and Charles, Abby, their children, and Charles's father, Robert. This new community was the personal creation of these people— their gifts, skills, and capacities, and their strong relationships that grew as they worked together.

Every neighborhood today has the assets of those first settlers: the gifts, skills, and capacities of each of the residents, and the power to establish working relationships that also allow us to find our way. So, like the pioneers, we start community building in our neighborhood by *using* our gifts, our skills, and our capacities.

The pioneers' process can help guide us. Like us, their families were imperfect, limited people. Mary was a bitter person. Sam was given to too much drink. Their oldest boy, John, had a shriveled left leg from birth. The younger boy, Peter, they called "slow." He would never learn how to read or count money.

Charles had lost his right arm in a mill accident back where they came from. Abby was tired all the time. Their teenage daughter, Jane, often drifted away in her mind and forgot what she was doing. Charles's father, Robert, had a hard time walking.

These were the people who created a homestead and a hometown. They each had clear problems, limitations, and dilemmas. But they had a clear priority: We must create a community. And so it was that they set aside their deficiencies and instead focused upon their capacities.

Sam knew carpentry. Mary had known weaving from childhood. John was a tireless worker in spite of his heavy limp. And little Peter loved tools. Charles could do any kind of ironwork and was a crack shot. Abby knew the Bible by heart and could preserve any kind of food. Jane sang beautifully and loved to make a garden. And old Robert had a mind full of know-how about nearly everything.

■ The Point

Mary, Sam, Charles, Abby, and Robert, along with their children, built their community out of either what they had or what they had known before. They created those properties that constitute community:

Gifts: Recognizing every capacity of everyone and using them to make a new way. By choice or by necessity, the pioneers set their needs, problems, and deficiencies aside.

Association: They voluntarily joined with other families to create what was better done together.

Hospitality: The welcoming of strangers. They needed strangers to join them, as the strangers brought knowledge and capacities that the host group did not have.

This is not to idealize that life, for there was violence, war, and all of the shadow side of every human society. It is to say that they were fortified to deal with the harshness of life through their talents and their connectedness with others.

▨ *Community Abundance Is Its Gifts*

Creating competence starts with making visible the gifts of everyone in the neighborhood—the families, the young people, the old people, the vulnerable people, the troublesome people. Everyone. We do this not out of altruism, but to create the elements of a satisfying life.

For example, we could identify the gifts, skills, and capacities of the people in the neighborhood. Here is a list of the ones that people in most neighborhoods would have:

Carpentry	Internet knowledge
Writing poetry	Listening
Driving a truck	Math
Game playing: chess, backgammon	Auto repair
Organizing ability	Gardening
Singing	Haircutting
Wallpapering	Making videos

Babysitting	House painting
Accounting	Bartending
Soccer	Artistic abilities
Cooking	Pruning trees
Fitness knowledge	Sitting with the old or the ill
Health remedies	Sewing

This is the short list. The challenge is to make these gifts visible among all in the neighborhood. These are the means for creating our social fabric. The task is to make more widely available these gifts in service of our core concerns for the child, the land, enterprise, food, health, the vulnerable, and our safety. With the consciousness and ability to connect our gifts and make them practical and usable, we experience what we are calling community abundance.

■ Making Gifts Visible

When we and the other neighbors know of each other's gifts, new community possibilities emerge. For example, the community can play an important role in rearing children and helping them to learn about their own abilities and what it means to be a contributing member of society. We can do the following:

- Have young people teach the Internet to seniors and adults.

- Hold gatherings where youth learn about music, painting, poetry, storytelling, and dance from artistic neighbors.

- Create a tutor list so that young people can learn what the neighbors know.

- Make an inventory of each neighbor's job, and then connect our teens to people with interesting jobs so that they can learn what the neighbors do and how to prepare for a vocation.

- Have a children's clothes exchange.

- Have rewards for older children tutoring younger children.

- Have monthly potluck dinners where we sing together and urge our children to share their talent with the adults.

Here are some ways that neighborhood gifts can help us care for the land:

- Bring broken things together to be repaired instead of making more waste.

- Have neighborhood hikes.

- Create neighborhood gardens. Join community-supported agriculture.

- Have a forum where people learn about buying local food and food security.

- Share transportation to work. Carpool with neighbors to schools, activities.

- Only buy things with no packaging.

There are many things to do to support a local economy and economic self-sufficiency:

- Help repair a neighbor's house. A modern barn raising.

- On the neighborhood website bulletin board, neighbors can post job openings in their workplaces.

- Identify the neighborhood entrepreneurs and convene them to share insights. They can offer advice to neighbors who want to start a business.

- Identify home businesses, and publicize and patronize them.

- At a neighborhood forum, invite local businesspeople to make presentations, and then develop a neighborhood compact to support the local businesses as well as new entrepreneurs from the neighborhood.

- At another forum, have neighborhood professionals, nurses, teachers, contractors inform us about what we need to know to "decode" their trades.

- Create a barter exchange where people can offer and receive skills such as haircutting, paperhanging, and minor electrical work. This is done with the belief that it will even out in the end.

- We can buy and eat locally produced and marketed food.

To provide more security, care, and health in the neighborhood, we can do the following:

- Create mutual support groups for single parents, bereaved neighbors, parents of teenagers, and people in other situations where the wisdom of common experience can help us make our way.

- Hold a forum on neighborhood security to get eyes on the street. Agree on who can pay attention at what times. Include a way of reporting on what police activity is in the neighborhood.

- Learn from peacemakers how to ease family and neighborhood quarrels.

- Have a forum to help us get organized and ask those who are home a lot to tell us what is happening.

- Connect child care with the elderly and retired. Find ways that children and the elderly can support each other and be less lonely. Help the mothers get some rest.

- Have a health exchange where people talk about what is working to stay healthy and deal with the aches and pains of life.

Now we are on our way to creating a culture of community. By naming and exchanging our individual gifts, capacities, and skills, we open new possibilities for the family and neighborhood to produce the satisfaction their own way.

■ The Power of Our Gifts

When we choose to make visible the gifts of those around us, we discover several things.

First, working together we begin to take creative responsibility for our families and our lives. We begin to make our neighborhood safer, healthier, wiser, richer, and a much better place to raise a family. Instead of feeling alone and overwhelmed by our family dilemmas, we begin to connect with other parents, children, youth, and seniors by extending our families. We feel the comfort, help, pleasure, and tangible support from those surrounding us.

Second, as we share gifts, all kinds of new connections and relationships are created. We cross lines once drawn between youth and adults, parents and children, seniors and juniors, the frail and the able. We become a competent community, a group of specially related people.

Third, we begin to understand the limits of money. Our community inventions usually cost little to nothing, and yet they become treasures. We see that you can't buy more safety, health, wisdom, or wealth. But together we can create them. We feel less burdened financially and less dependent on outside institutions. We are finding the citizen way.

Fourth, as we create the future together, we find a new kind of trust emerging. Our neighbors become people we can count on. And they count on us. A profound sense of security begins to emerge.

Fifth, we feel powerful. We find our own way, and that sense of power leads us to hold celebrations, acclaiming our successes while recognizing our frailties and those among us who have passed away.

Finally, we begin to create a history together. We can tell our story: We know how to join in educating our children. We have learned how to engage our old people. We write our own story, and we would love to share it with your neighborhood because we also can learn from your way.

▦ Connected Gifts Create Associations

Of the three properties of an abundant community, we turn our attention again to the second: association. Gifts become useful when they are connected to the gifts of others. Connected citizens are in association and create associational life. This certain kind of connecting is the key to creating abundance in community.

Associational connections have several benefits:

- The giver sees their own value in the appreciation of the receiver.

- The receiver sees the value of the giver in the gift.

■ The community becomes more valuable as the value of the gift is shared to benefit others.

However, many neighborhoods share a common dilemma. Since people and their gifts are not connected, and the neighborhood is filled with isolated people and families living alone, who or what will initiate the connection of gifts in our neighborhood?

Here, we can return to the pioneer families and see how they proceeded. As soon as there were enough new settlers around the original families, they all gathered together in small groups to undertake tasks that a family couldn't accomplish on its own.

Several families shared their labor, pulling stumps and raising barns. Homemakers joined together to share information on weaving, gardening, and cooking. Farmers joined in sharing information about the best way to grow crops on this new land. Many parents created a group to locate and start a new school. Other families of the same faith joined together for weekly worship. Some musical people joined together and created a choir.

Whatever vision they had or necessity they felt, a small group was created to bring it to life. And through the formation of these small groups, a community was created. Because of their joint efforts, a culture not only of gifts but of associational life was created.

A brilliant observer of how North American communities were created was the young French count we introduced in chapter 4, Alexis de Tocqueville. In 1831, he traveled to cities, towns, villages, and settlements in Canada and the United States. All over. He was amazed to see how communities were created anew on prairies and in forests. He concluded that the key to those community creations was the hundreds of small groups that the pioneers formed. They were the essential community building blocks of pioneer Americans and Canadians.

When de Tocqueville returned to France, he wrote about the community-building process that he had observed. He titled the book *Democracy in America* and focused especially on the small groups of newly connected neighbors. He named these groups "associations." They were the small, face-to-face groups of local people who took on thousands of missions— and they were not paid.

He reported,

> Americans of all ages, all conditions, and all dispositions, constantly form associations. They have . . . associations of a thousand kinds, religious, moral, serious, futile, general or restricted, enormous or diminutive. The Americans make associations to give entertainments, to found seminaries, to build inns, to construct churches, to diffuse books, to send missionaries to the antipodes; in this manner they found hospitals, prisons and schools. If it is proposed to inculcate some truth, or to foster some feeling by the encouragement of a great example, they form an association. Wherever at the head of some new undertaking you see the government in France, or a man of rank in England, in the United States you will be sure to find an association.[26]

And he concluded that

> [N]othing, in my opinion, is more deserving of our attention than the intellectual and moral associations [of North America]. . . . We understand them imperfectly, because we have hardly ever seen anything of the kind. . . . In democratic countries the science of association is the mother of science; the progress of all the rest depends upon the progress it has made. Among the laws that rule human societies there is one that seems to be more precise and clear than all the others. If men are to remain civilized, or to become so, the art of associating together must grow and improve in the same ratio in which the equality of conditions is increased.[27]

■ *The Power of Associations*

De Tocqueville was one of the first to recognize that our associations were central to our democracy. Voting, he observed, is vital, but it is the power to give your power away—that is, to delegate your will to a representative. An association, on the other hand, is a means to make power rather than giving it away. This new associational tool involved using these community powers:

- The power to decide *what* needs to be done. This power is not delegated to experts. It is based upon the belief that local citizens, connected together, have the special ability to know what needs doing in their community.

- The power to decide *how* we could do what needs to be done. Here again, local knowledge is the basic expertise.

- The power to *join* with one's neighbors to do what needs to be done.

The association is the tool that allows us to produce the future we envision. A citizen is a person with the awesome power to determine and create a common future. And so it is that the association makes citizenship possible. It empowers us because neighbors can decide what needs to be done and how it can be done—and, of greatest importance, they are the people who can do it.

In associations we are not consumers. We are not clients. We are citizens with gifts and the power to make powerful communities.

■ Associations Today

It has been nearly two centuries since de Tocqueville named the unique associational heart of North American communities. It is our good fortune that we are still the earth's most associational people. If each of our neighbors would itemize the associations he or she belongs to or participates in, we would probably find that we would have a list of fifty to one hundred groups. They would be groups of every kind. A list of the kinds of associations that neighbors are typically involved in would include all the resources we need to fulfill what is satisfying—from caring for our children to ensuring our safety, expressing our compassion, caring for animals, protecting the earth, you name it.

The list below gets specific about the kinds of associations we are talking about. Each occupies that space between what a family can do and what more organized systems are engaged in. These are mostly volunteer groups that rise and fall based purely on the interests of those who choose to show up:

- **Addiction prevention and recovery groups**
  Testimonial Group for Addicts
  Campaign for a Drug-Free Neighborhood

- **Advisory community support groups (friends of . . .)**
  Friends of the Library
  Neighborhood Park Advisory Council

■ **Animal care groups**
Conservation Association
Humane Society

■ **Anticrime groups**
Children's Safe Haven Neighborhood Group
Senior Safety Group

■ **Business organizations/support groups**
Jaycees
Neighborhood Business Association

■ **Charitable groups and drives**
Local Hospital Auxiliary

■ **Civic events groups**
Committees to celebrate holidays
Health Fair Committee

■ **Cultural groups**
Community Choir
Drama Club

■ **Disability/special needs groups**
Parents of Disabled Children

■ **Education groups**
Local book clubs

■ **Elderly groups**
Retired Executives Club
Church Seniors Club

■ **Environmental groups**
Neighborhood Recycling Club
Save the Park Committee

■ **Family support groups**
Teen Parent Organization
Parent Alliance Group

■ **Health advocacy and fitness groups**
Neighborhood Health Council
Senior Fitness Club

■ **Heritage groups**
Neighborhood Historical Society
Ethnic Heritage Association
Hobby and collectors' groups
Arts and Crafts Club
Garden Club of Neighbors

■ **Men's groups**
Church men's organizations
Men's sports organizations

■ **Mentoring groups**
After-school mentors
Church Mentoring Group

■ **Mutual support groups**
La Leche League
Family-to-family groups

■ **Neighborhood improvement groups**
Council of Block Clubs
Neighborhood Safety Group

■ **Recreation groups**
Bowling League
Little League
Town Soccer League

■ **Residents' associations**
Block clubs
Tenants' associations

■ **Service clubs**
Zonta
Rotary Clubs

■ **Social groups**
Card-Playing Club
Dance clubs

■ **Social cause/advocacy issue groups**
Community Action Council
Soup Kitchen Group

■ **Veterans' groups**
Veterans of Foreign Wars (VFW)
Women's veterans' organizations

■ **Women's groups**
Women's sports groups
Eastern Star
Sororities

■ **Youth groups**
4-H
Teen Leadership Club

It is telling that despite the large number of groups we are involved in, associational life takes a backseat to professional and system life. We may have a chamber of commerce that is proud of its five thousand members in a good-sized city, yet there is no parallel group that promotes or even counts the number of associations. We treat them as tangential to what constitutes a community. Associational life ranks well behind our interest in business, sports, the arts and entertainment, and commercial or residential real estate development.

■ *Associations Are the Workhorses of Communities*

Associations are important because if we want to wean ourselves away from our dependence on the consumer economy and lifestyle, associational life gives us one powerful means to do this. In addition to the gifts and skills of local residents, associations are the second major tool available for community building and fulfilling our desire for satisfaction.

Associations have three major roles in helping us to produce a satisfying life of our own making.

First, many are engaged in work that supports what matters most to citizens and thereby strengthens community life. For example:

■ The Parents of Disabled Children are broadening the opportunities for all children to learn and play together.

■ The neighborhood Park Council is guiding the local park manager in developing the park to engage the diverse interests of local residents.

■ The Drama Club is involving neighbors in theater and entertaining the neighborhood.

■ The Seniors' Club is involving local schoolchildren in their inter-generational initiative.

■ The Garden Club has transformed the vacant lot into a refreshing green space.

■ The Softball League has a project to mentor local youth.

■ The Veterans of Foreign Wars are organizing the annual patriotic celebration.

Indeed, every local association is strengthening the local community by bringing neighbors together to use their powers as citizens. Every association also counts on volunteers to make it work.

Many associations take on new community roles that reach beyond their primary function. We see this broadening of functions in many groups:

■ The Lions Club collects used eyeglasses to distribute in less-privileged communities.

■ The local union collects toys each year from its members to give to neighboring children.

■ The Westside Seniors Club creates a literacy initiative to assist immigrant neighbors.

■ The Drama Club produces a play for local residents that advocates recycling and other "green" practices at home.

■ Several bowling leagues raise money to equip a new neighborhood "tot lot."

- The Garden Club, following the vision of two members, creates a family movie night in the local park.

- A local political club sponsors a monthly children's clothing exchange for the neighborhood.

Finally, if we look beyond the association's name, we see that many are involved in additional, secondary activities that produce a significant community benefit. In fact, if we identified all the associations our neighbors are involved in and identified the basic functions of these groups as well as the additional community benefit activities, we would uncover the same foundation of our community that de Tocqueville discovered in 1831.

■ Associations of Associations

Many associations strengthen their local community in another way. This occurs when several of them join together to create a neighborhood association to improve the lives of all the residents. These *associations of associations* have proved to be the most powerful tool for creating a community of abundance. The reason is clear. Every association is empowering and powerful, because it acts as the amplifier of the gifts, skills, and talents of each member. It is the principal community means of helping people to give their gifts.

As each association makes its members more powerful, in the same way an association of associations greatly amplifies the power of each association, which makes each individual member more powerful in turn.

Community means "people in relationship." *Association* means "people in powerful relationship." A competent community finds its own way through ever-increasing connections between people who exercise their right of freedom of association in order to create a better future together. If we understand the potential place of associations in community building, we can act on what we know to produce something different from what we have.

7 ■ The Power of Connectors

BUILDING COMMUNITY COMPETENCE depends on initiatives that result in more individual connections and more associational connections. The basic question is how to multiply the connections and associations in the modern world we live in. The answer begins with those who have the capacity to connect others in our current neighborhoods. We call these people *community connectors.* In answering the question of what action we can take to create more abundant communities, we want to elevate and make more visible people who have this connecting capacity. We also want to encourage each of us to discover the connecting possibility in our own selves.

We can't hire a community connector. There is no degree in community connecting, and we are not advocates for one. It is not taught by the academy, which is fortunate, for that means it has not been curricularized, certified, managed, or adopted by a system. So, who will do the connecting? What about us? We are as likely as any other neighbor to be a connector or have the potential to become one.

■ The Vital Role of Connectors

Making connections is a skill often underused, undeveloped, or unrecognized. But it is a natural skill and abundant in every neighborhood.

The key to becoming a competent community, then, is simply a matter of intention—an intention to enhance the spirit and culture of connecting.

The operating question becomes, who are the proven and potential connectors of our acquaintance? Who sees the gifts of local people and figures out ways to share them? Whom do people turn to when something needs to be done on the block? Who are the people who take responsibility for civic events? Who are the leaders of our local associations? Who took the initiative to create a new neighborhood group to solve a problem or carry out a vision?

These are the proven connectors. Some may be called leaders. Most will not, because compared with a leader, a connector has a very different role in the community. A leader is a person at the front of the room who acts as a voice for the community. A connector is in the center of the room, often unrecognized but always creating new relationships and often acting in a modest way.

We can specify what characteristics connectors have in common in hopes that you are one or know one:

- They are "gift-centered" people. They see the "full half" in everyone.

- They are well connected themselves, active in associational and civic life. They know the ways of their neighborhood.

- They are trusted and create new trusting relationships. The trust they have grows from the fact that they see the gift of their neighbors, and they are willing contributors to their neighbors and the neighborhood.

- They believe in the people in their community. They are not cynical, doubting observers of local residents. They know that their community is rich in resources.

- And they are people who get joy from connecting, convening, and inviting people to come together. They are not seeking to lead people. They know the power in joining people. They are hospitable.

What is required of us is to take an imaginary walk around our neighborhood and ask, "Who are the connectors?" Sometimes they come in special forms. They might be a little nosy or noisy, or have a few opinions, but these are simply ways to identify them. If we are to support a gift-centered world, then we value the gifts of our connectors.

To give an example, we introduce you to DeAmon Harges. He is a member of Broadway United Methodist Church in Indianapolis. DeAmon spends many of his days simply walking his neighborhood, knocking on doors, talking to people. He is armed with a smile, an interest in others, and three basic questions. He asks neighbors, "Who do you know? What do you know that would be useful to others? Are you willing to teach what you know?"

He also has an intuitive knowledge of what makes a community competent. When asked what the neighborhood way is, he says, "We pass our children around. We find our fathers on street corners and alleyways. Any of those men could be my father. These men are the fathers of my brothers and sisters." He does not mean this literally; he is saying that his neighbors help raise every child, and what he does is keep the neighbors connected.

There is a DeAmon in every neighborhood. They are all ages, seniors to teenagers. They have lived here a long time and they just moved in. They are the foundation of community transformation. All we have to do is look.

A Table for Connectors

One way we can begin to discover the power of our families and neighborhood is to invite the local connectors to come together and share their successes and ideas by forming a Connectors' Table. They can then discuss questions like, what new connections of neighbors and associations would make a better neighborhood? Who are the people with connector potential who could be invited to join the Table? Are there senior connectors at the Table? Are there teen connectors involved?

This core group can become initiators of a new community culture as they consciously pursue the connective possibilities they envision. To begin, people at this Connectors' Table can identify the gifts and skills of all the neighbors—the gold in the community treasure chest. They can ask four simple questions of each neighbor as they identify the neighborhood treasures:

- What are your gifts of the head? What do you especially know about—birds, mathematics, neighborhood history?

- What are your gifts of the hands? What do you know about doing things—baseball, carpentry, cooking, guitar, gardening?

- What are your gifts of the heart? What do you especially care about—children, the environment, elders, veterans, politics?

- What clubs, groups, and associations do you and your family belong to or participate in?

This is the conversation that begins the process of connection, which is what gives people the alternative to look outside the family for satisfaction. We could say that connection is the antidote to consumption. It begins with identifying the neighborhood treasures waiting to be given.

■ Connecting Individual Gifts

The Connectors' Table can begin to see how these gifts of the head, hands, and heart can be brought together in new relationships. They will learn some fascinating things:

- Charles knows how to juggle. Who are the neighborhood kids that would love to learn from him?

- Sue, Mary, Charlene, and Diane all have young children and are willing to swap babysitting. They don't know each other, so we can connect the four of them.

- Twenty-two people play musical instruments—alone. They can be connected to start a community or neighborhood band—maybe two.

- Seven people care especially about the environment. Connected, they could develop a plan to engage the neighbors in renewing the deteriorated local park.

- Three people say they know how to start a business. They can be introduced to Sam, Sarah, and Joan, who say they want to start a business.

■ Jane, Nancy, and Devonte care about health. They can be connected to create a healthy-neighborhood initiative.

■ Twenty-nine people have all kinds of skills relating to home maintenance and repair. They can become a neighborhood home adviser group, available when neighbors need work done on their houses.

The idea of a Connectors' Table is meant literally and also as a metaphor for what makes a family more functional, a community more competent. The Connectors' Table represents a form of inquiry, an inquiry into the gifts of the family and neighborhood.

Once this inquiry begins, we begin to develop the power to create satisfaction. The power to raise a child, get healthier, be safer, nurture a local economy and its food. This moves the idea of a functional family and an abundant community from a vision or ideal to an experience. This is what turns a consumer into a citizen.

■ Connecting Associations

As the Table members make these connections, they are often creating new associations. Because of their connections, they also know the names of the associations with which the neighbors are active. They will discover more than anyone in the neighborhood imagined.

This associational treasure chest provides the Connectors' Table with many new possibilities:

First, they can see which residents might be connected to the existing associations. If there are four choirs, which people who like to sing can be connected to them? Which teenagers can be connected to associations of adults so that they can learn the way of community and citizenship? The young people could become members of environmental groups, hobby groups, men's and women's organizations, neighborhood block clubs, geek clubs.

Second, appropriate associations can be connected to the newly connected neighbors. For example, if the new environmental group focuses on park renewal, it could be joined or assisted by men's and women's groups, faith groups, the neighborhood historical society, and fitness groups.

Third, if some group in the neighborhood focuses on any issue or vision, all the associations can be first notified and asked if they wish to participate. Which associations will help with the holiday celebration or the neighborhood picnic? We want a new clubhouse in the park: Which associations will help raise the money; which will help build it? Who is willing to work to save some houses in foreclosure and find eventual owners for them?

Fourth, and perhaps of greatest importance, the members of the Connectors' Table can meet with the president or chairperson of each association and find out the following:

- What community benefit activities is the association presently engaged in?

- What kinds of new neighborhood initiatives would their members be willing to join? Would they help with efforts to improve health, safety, youth, the environment?

- Would they be willing to join with all the other local groups in creating a new neighborhood association of associations to make the neighborhood a better place in which to live and prosper?

The answer to this last question is most important of all. For an association of associations is the most a powerful force for re-creating an abundant neighborhood. While each association has a particular focus that is usually not the whole neighborhood, in an association of associations, each group adds its power to the vision of a better neighborhood. In this way, disconnected associations of diverse interests become the unified neighborhood force for a new way for citizens to produce their own future.

The Connectors' Table becomes transforming when it has initiated new relationships between individual neighbors, between neighbors and associations, and between associations. Each connection is an asset that has been invested through connections. And the sum of the connections is a community that is wealthy in security, health, wisdom, and enterprise.

Welcoming Strangers

One dilemma, however, faces even neighborhoods with a wealth of invested gifts and transformed associations. It is the dilemma of the outsider—the outsider in the neighborhood and the outsider outside the neighborhood.

Usually, the outsiders in the neighborhood are the people who have names that tell about their problem. Remember the pioneer families? Sam, a father, drank too much. Mary was a little sharp. Their boy John was born with a shriveled leg. And his brother, Peter, was "slow" to learn and never did learn how to read. Charles, the father of the other family, had one arm. His wife, Abby, was constantly fatigued. Their daughter, Jane, was mentally fragile. And Charles's father was feeble and found it hard to walk.

But each of them also had gifts, capacities, and skills. They used them to create the very community where you now live—in spite of their deficits, needs, and problems.

The same is true of our own neighborhood. While we all have deficiencies and problems, some of our neighbors get labeled by their deficiencies or condition. They are given names like mentally ill, physically disabled, developmentally disabled, youth-at-risk, single mom, welfare recipient, cranky, loner, trailer court person, immigrant, low income.

All of these people have gifts we need for a really strong community. And many of them desperately need to be asked to join and contribute. Their only real deficiency is the lack of connection to the rest of us. And our greatest community weakness is the fact that we haven't seen them and felt their loneliness. We have often ignored or even feared them. And yet their gifts are our greatest undiscovered treasure!

Therefore, the Connectors' Table needs to pay special attention to the people at the edge, the people with the names that describe their empty half rather than their gifted full half. The connectors are motivated by the fact that historically, every great local community has engaged the talents of every single member. For the strength of our neighborhood is greatest when we all give all our gifts.

This means that the key words for our community are *invitation*, *participation*, and *connection*. We each need to become great inviters, like a host or hostess, opening the door to our community life. Our goal will be to have everyone participating, giving and receiving gifts. And our method will be connection—introducing the newly discovered gifts to the other neighbors and associations.

The great Irish poet William Butler Yeats is credited with an aphorism to guide the connectors: "There are no strangers here; only friends you haven't yet met." So perhaps the best description of an abundant neighborhood, a powerful neighborhood, a great community is one that welcomes those on the margin, which is the heart of hospitality.

■ Outsiders beyond Our Community Borders

What about the outsider outside our neighborhood? The foreigner who lives on the other side of Halsted Street, the boundary of our neighborhood; or the person outside the neighborhood who prays on a rug five times a day; or the outsider who lives in a neighborhood where people park their cars on the lawn and repair them on the street; or the rich man who doesn't want to live among us.

The truth is that every local community of any kind is a group of specially connected people. But the very fact of their special connection necessarily creates outsiders. An association of Labrador retriever owners, without intention, makes outsiders of poodle owners. And every neighborhood necessarily creates outsiders by establishing boundaries. The question is, what kind of boundary is it? Is it a boundary of superiority and exclusion, a dangerous place to approach? Or is it the edge of a place that has a welcome at the door?

The challenge is to keep expanding the limits of our hospitality. Our willingness to welcome strangers. This welcome is the sign of a community confident in itself. It has nothing to fear from the outsider. The outsider has gifts, insights, and experiences to share for our benefit. So we look forward to sharing our culture, gifts, and associations with others. "Come on in. What would you like to eat? We have a great community band we want you to hear. And let us show you our new park that we created ourselves."

The beautiful, remarkable sign of a secure community is that it has a welcome at the edge. And who better than the Connectors' Table to remind us, should we forget, that there are important connections to be made beyond our borders? For beyond them are people who need our gifts, as we need theirs. The only thing we have to fear in our community is fear of outsiders.

■ Dealing with Our Reluctance

Discovering the gifts of our neighbors sounds easy. But because many of us live in isolation from those on our block, we become reluctant to intrude into other people's lives. We don't want to be viewed as eccentric, which might lead to further isolation.

In some neighborhoods, we might feel unsafe knocking on the door of someone we do not know. Whatever the situation, fear of rejection is a powerful deterrent to connection. Especially for those of us who feel more introverted.

We might think of our reluctance to approach a neighbor as similar to our fear of public speaking. For those who have chosen to overcome this fear, the shift starts when we begin to believe that people out there are waiting for us to speak. It happens when we redefine the anxiety of speaking as excitement and realize that moving toward the anxiety is enlivening, in fact a wake-up call we have been waiting for. The courage it takes to rebuild the fabric of our community is the price we pay for creating a world we want to inhabit. In the end, the way to get past our discomfort is to do it again and again and again.

Finding Our Own Way

Even though we have discussed the role of connectors, those people who naturally gravitate toward bringing people together, discovering the abundance of a community needs to be within the reach of each of us. Here are some thoughts on how each of us can begin to find our way into the heart of community and toward an effective neighborhood.

- **Go with someone else.** Invite someone you know in the neighborhood who will join you. Better yet if the person is already good at meeting strangers. The shift in the function of the family and the competence of the community really begins with this first invitation. We might even say that the transformation has occurred the moment we ask another to join us in creating a community.

- **Focus on gifts.** Experience shows that people will be flattered by your interest in their gifts. People are waiting to be asked to contribute if what you want to ask for is something they want to do, something they are interested in doing. You are going to find that it is fun and fulfilling when you talk to your neighbors about their gifts. They are waiting for you because nobody has asked before. You are contributing to the community by giving it an opportunity to give its gifts.

■ **Practice.** Rehearse the conversation with the partner you have recruited to join you. Here is an example of what you might say as you knock on the door of your neighbor. You can try this on for size and then customize it:

> YOU: I live across the street, and I am one of your neighbors. This is Diane, who lives two doors down. Some of us on the block are thinking about how we can get together and improve things. We are concerned about supporting the kids in this neighborhood. (Or green space, or the local economy, or whatever is on your mind. We will just use young people for the example.) Your neighbor, Mrs. Jones, said you were the kind of person who has good ideas and talents. So she said we should talk to you. Could we come in and talk about the neighborhood for a few minutes?

> NEIGHBOR: What do you have in mind?

> YOU: We don't know each other that well on this block, but we have begun to find out that a lot of people have different skills, gifts, and interests; and we are trying to find out what those are, so that we can begin to see how people can share them. Especially with young people.

> NEIGHBOR: Well, I don't have any kids.

> YOU: That doesn't mean you don't have something to offer the kids who are here on the block. When you think about yourself, how would you describe the things you know about, the gifts and skills you have, and the things you love to do?

> NEIGHBOR: I like to garden, read, and walk my dog. But everybody does these. Besides, I am busy.

> YOU: What kind of gardening do you do? What do you like to read?

NEIGHBOR: I grow roses. I read about World War II.

YOU: Well, I like growing flowers. So does Mr. Smith. There are other people on this block who are interested in gardening. A couple of kids on the block have gardening as a school project. Would you be willing to join your neighbors in showing the kids how? About your interest in World War II, we have several high school kids who are studying this and have to do papers. Often they are not too interested. If we got two or three together, would you talk to them about World War II? You might really get them interested.

NEIGHBOR: Well, possibly.

YOU: Let me get back to you. When is the best time to contact you? Let me ask the kids. Also, are there any other neighbors you think we might want to talk to? We're interested in their skills or interests in any area. A couple of final questions: Is there anything you would like to learn about? And could you tell me about the clubs or groups to which you belong?

■ **Start small.** We suggest you start by talking to five people. One at a time. Don't begin by calling a meeting. Begin by meeting people door to door. It is more personal, and you will learn more.

■ **Consider the possibilities.** After talking to five people, sit down with your partner and review everything you learned about the first person you interviewed.

Make a list of the possibilities you both see for connecting that person's gifts and interests with other people in the neighborhood, including youth. Do the two of you know people with an interest in gardening? Would any of the people you interviewed like to learn about gardening? Who would teach about gardening?

■ **Keep going.** Then do the same for each of the other four people. If no connection appears, keep interviewing until a match occurs.

■ **Make connections.** Decide how the two of you are going to connect the gifts of one of these people. How will we introduce one of the people we interviewed to another person or two who could usefully receive their gifts?

■ **Review and reflect.** Discuss with your co-conspirator what you are learning about inviting others, seeking their gifts, connecting those in the neighborhood. What have you learned? What works?

■ *Making Community Abundance Visible*

This simple process can be extended over time to help build the strength of your community. Points to keep in mind:

■ In its simplest form, the process is connecting individuals to individuals. As the effort grows, you can use the interviews to connect two people and begin a gardening club or a history club. Or a food club, a local marketplace for barter exchange, a group caring for those on the margin, a health support group, a safe-neighborhood group. This is how associations begin.

■ You can connect an individual to an existing association. Is there already a gardening group in the neighborhood, and can you connect people there?

■ You can also do it the other way around—for example, connect the gardening club to individuals and initiatives in the neighborhood where the gardening club can help. Say there are six teenagers or seniors or other residents who want to learn how to garden. By putting them together, you are broadening the association constituencies so that they are becoming more active in creating a better neighborhood.

■ You can link association to association. You can say to the gardening club that there is an environmental club here. Do you think the gardening club would meet with the environmental club to preserve the neighborhood and its beauty? Or can you connect the gardening club with people who like to cook?

Then, out of all these efforts, you will find there are some who enjoy connecting, and you can invite them to join in the interview process. You begin to add people to the Connectors' Table we are creating.

This process enhances the community-building efforts that already exist, like block parties, clean-ups, picnics. These are social events, and now what we seek is to build deeper relationships by collecting people's gifts and providing a means through which the gifts can be offered to their neighbors. Here we want to be explicit about how this process can return power to the family and the neighborhood.

■ Example: When a Village Raises a Child

In every neighborhood, the issue that all can come together around is a concern for the next generation. This is what the village is primarily needed for. The question that begins to construct a village is, what does each person in the neighborhood have to offer? How can the adults, with their skills and knowledge, be connected to the young people in the neighborhood? And how can the gifts and interests of young people be connected to adults?

We asked a group of neighbors what they would do (or are doing) to care for the next generation. Here are some of their answers.

■ First, we have to know the children. We have to decide to know the names of each child in the neighborhood.

■ Second, we have to know the parents of the children who are around us. The children in most neighborhoods are better organized and connected than the adults. We have to catch up with them.

■ Third, we have to know that each adult has a gift or passion that can be connected to young people.

■ Fourth, we need to know what each child knows, cares about, and wants to learn about or teach adults or other children.

■ Finally, our goal is to have each child know what they are good at. This becomes a collective purpose of the family and neighbors.

We need this information if we really mean it when we say that it takes a village to raise a child. Now, all we need is neighbors who are willing to make the connections. You are one of those neighbors.

■ The Story of an Abundant Community

We began the book by detailing the emotional and social costs of the consumer society—how it is designed for dissatisfaction. We discussed the limitations of systems resulting from their devotion to scale and replicability and their uneasiness with all that is personal.

We have been discussing a way for families and neighbors together to create that part of life that systems can never provide. And this life is created from the abundance of our gifts, the expansion of our associations, and our willingness to extend an invitation to those we have not known.

We end with a story of how this works. It is not one story but a composite of several—the real-life experiences of citizens from neighborhoods around the world that we have worked with. The names have been changed to protect those guilty of fully discovering what it means to be a citizen and a neighbor.

■ HOW NEIGHBORS CREATED THEIR OWN COMMUNITY

It all began when Naomi Alessio and Jackie Barton, two mothers on the block, were complaining to each other about how overwhelming life seemed: work, meals, lessons, school, and especially the kids. Things were out of hand. Except, Naomi noted, that her son, Theron, had begun to turn around. It was because of old Mr. Thompson down the block. He had some kind of shop in his garage where he made things out of metal. Last summer, Theron was walking down the alley, and Mr. Thompson's garage door was open. He stopped to watch Mr. Thompson at work, and the old man invited him in. Something clicked. Theron began to stop by every day after school, and he started bringing home metal pieces he had made on a lathe and a forge.

Naomi said she could see Theron change. He was proud of what he made. And Mr. Thompson even paid him to make a few things. Naomi especially liked the fact that she had stopped worrying about Theron's after-school activities.

Jackie said maybe she should introduce her son, Alvin, to Mr. Thompson. Alvin was in trouble. Naomi felt two boys would overwhelm Mr. Thompson and Theron would lose out, so she said there might be other people in the neighborhood who did something that would interest Alvin.

They began to think about the other men on the block. They knew that Gerald Lilly was into fishing big time and that Sam Wheatley was a saxophonist, but that was about it. Jackie thought that it would be good if they knew what each man's special skill was, so that all their sons could be involved.

However, they didn't feel comfortable going by themselves to meet with the men, so they told Mr. Thompson about their idea and asked if he'd go with them. He said he'd love to go. He had lots of free time.

It took them about three weeks to visit all the men on the block in the evenings. When they were done, they were amazed, and even proud, at what they had found. There were men who knew juggling, barbecuing, bookkeeping, hunting, cutting hair, bowling, investigating crimes, writing poems, fixing cars, weightlifting, church-type singing, teaching dogs tricks, mathematics, praying, and how to play trumpet, drums, and sax.

The men knew so much that Naomi, Jackie, and Mr. Thompson thought there were some girls, as well as boys, on the block who would want to learn from the men. Because they now knew all the men, they could see it would be pretty easy to connect them to the interested kids.

While they were meeting the men, there were three—Charles Wilt, Mark Sutter, and Sonny Reed—who showed a real interest in what they were doing. They recruited all three to join in visiting all the families to find out which things the men knew that interested particular kids. With that information, they could make a match.

It was Mark Sutter who first had the idea that everyone else quickly adopted. When he visited his first family and talked with the kids, one said he was interested in computers and already knew a lot about them. Mark realized that he needed to learn more about computers, and he was sure that several of the other men would like to learn, too.

When the six visitors got together after their first interviews with the kids, Mark told about the boy who knew about computers. He said it made him realize that they ought to ask all the kids what they knew about, just like they had done with the men. That way, they could match the kids' knowledge to the adults, just as they planned to match the kids to the men's interest.

When they were done talking to all the kids, they found they had twenty-two things the young people knew that might interest some adults or other kids on the block.

Once Naomi, Jackie, Mr. Thompson, Charles, Mark, and Sonny had finished visiting the men and all the children, it was easy to make the matches. Because of their visits, they knew everyone personally and saw how enthusiastic they were about sharing their skill with other people on the block.

As the six made their connections on the block, they became quite a team. They called themselves the Matchmakers, and as they got more experience, they began to see that often several neighbors had the same interests. Therefore, they began to match up those people in teams.

Over the next year, matching the interests of the neighbors, the Matchmakers created eight teams. There was a gardeners' team that shared growing tips and showed four other families and their kids how to create a garden—even on a flat rooftop! Several people worried about the bad economy. Once they were teamed up, they created a website for the block. To give it some flair, they found people in the neighborhood to take photos for the site.

Part of the site was designed to be used by neighbors who knew about jobs in their workplace. They could post this job information on the website. Sometimes they would introduce interested neighbors to the hiring people at their jobs.

When Jolene Cass saw the website, she posted one of her poems and asked if there were other poets on the block. It turned out there were three. They began to have coffee, share their writing, and post their better poems on the website.

So many people had musical talent that they formed the Block Band, made up of eleven members—adults and kids. The same happened with singers. The block now had a choir led by Sarah Ensley, an eighty-year-old woman with time on her hands.

It was Charles Dawes, a police officer, who formed the Safety Team, which joined adults and young people into several kinds of groups, ensuring that the block would be a safe haven for everyone.

Libby Green had lived on the block for seventy-four years. She knew a lot about its history, so the Matchmakers got two of the teens, Lenore Manse and Jim Caldwell, to write down her stories of the neighborhood's history. Then they posted the stories on the website. When they were finished, Lenore thought it would be good to write down each family's history. (She loved to write.) So, she persuaded Jim and her best friend, Lannie Eaton, to join in writing down the histories and rounding up photos to go along with them.

Then they were posted on the website. The six Matchmakers could see how interested the neighbors were in the family histories. And it occurred to Charles Wilt that the histories would be a good way to welcome new neighbors. The Matchmakers could give the newcomers a copy of the block history, get information about their family history, and find out about their interests and what they knew. That way, the Matchmakers could introduce the newcomers to the block through the website and begin to connect them with their neighbors.

After about two years, the block had a special history of its own. At the annual block party, one of the Matchmakers told the history, named the teams, and told about their work. And it was Jackie Barton, one of the founding mothers, who made the last speech. She said, "What we have done is broken all the lines. We broke the lines between the men. We broke the lines between the women. Then the lines were broken between the men and the women. And best of all, the lines were broken between the adults and the children and between all of us and our seniors. All the lines are broken; we're all connected, and we're a real community now."

The experience that embraces all we have been speaking of, the word that always appears at the end of every long and engaging encounter, is *love*.

A great community creates conditions where people can fall in love.
It is a place where we can make a fuss about one another.
A place where we can ask, "How did I ever live without you?"

—Lois Smidt, BeyondWelfare.org

▦ Notes

■ Introduction

1. Robert J. Sampson, papers derived from the ongoing "Project on Human Development in Chicago Neighborhoods," University of Michigan, Inter-university Consortium for Political and Social Research, http://www.icpsr.umich.edu/PHDCN/publications.html (accessed January 6, 2010).

■ Chapter 1: The Limits of Consumption

2. Wendell Berry, *The Unsettling of America: Culture and Agriculture* (San Francisco: Sierra Club Books, 1977), 19.
3. Ibid., 20.
4. Jeffrey Kaplan, "The Gospel of Consumption: And the Better Future We Left Behind," *Orion*, May/June 2008, http://www.orionmagazine.org/index.php/articles/article/2962 (accessed April 29, 2009).
5. Jane Jacobs, *The Death and Life of Great American Cities* (1961; reprint with new foreword by author, New York: Modern Library, 1993). See also *Dark Age Ahead* (New York: Random House, 2004) and "Healthy Cities, Urban Theory, and Design: The Power of Jane Jacobs," http://bss.sfsu.edu/pamuk/urban/.
6. Sampson, "Project on Human Development in Chicago Neighborhoods."
7. See, e.g., Elaina M. Kyrouz, Keith Humphreys, and Colleen Loomis, "A Review of Research on the Effectiveness of Self-Help Mutual Aid Groups," in *The Self-Help Group Sourcebook*, 7th ed., Barbara J. White and Edward Madara, eds. (Dover, NJ: American Self-Help Group Clearinghouse, 2002).

8. E.g., World Health Organization, *The Determinants of Health*, http://www.who .int/hia/evidence/doh/en/ (accessed January 3, 2010).

9. Robert D. Putnam, *Bowling Alone: The Collapse and Revival of American Community* (New York: Simon & Schuster, 2000). See also http://www.bowlingalone.com.

10. Robert D. Putnam, *Making Democracy Work: Civic Traditions in Modern Italy* (Princeton, NJ: Princeton University Press, 1992).

11. U.S. Department of Labor, Current Population Survey, Percent Using Job Search Methods, 2008.

■ Chapter 2: What Did We Lose and Where Did It Go?

12. Kaplan, "The Gospel of Consumption."

■ Chapter 3: The Effects of Living in a Consumer World

13. Kaplan, "The Gospel of Consumption."

14. Gerard F. Anderson, Peter S. Hussey, Bianca K. Frogner, and Hugh R. Waters, "Health Spending in the United States and the Rest of the Industrialized World," *Health Affairs*, July/August 2005; 24(4): 903–14.

15. Kaplan, "The Gospel of Consumption."

16. Hiroko Tabuchi, "When Consumers Cut Back: An Object Lesson from Japan," *New York Times,* February 21, 2009, http://www.nytimes.com/2009/02/22/ business/worldbusiness/22japan.html?_r=1 (accessed February 24, 2009).

17. Kaplan, "The Gospel of Consumption."

18. Ibid.

■ Chapter 5: Community Abundance in Action

19. Tabuchi, "When Consumers Cut Back."

20. Lionel Robbins, *An Essay on the Nature and Significance of Economic Science* (1932; 2nd ed. rev. and extended, London: Macmillan, 1945), 16, http://www.scribd .com/doc/14242989/An-Essay-on-the-Nature-and-Significance-of-Economic-Science-Lionel-Robbins (accessed February 24, 2009).

21. Mike Green, with Henry Moore and John O'Brien, *ABCD in Action: When People Care Enough to Act* (Toronto: Inclusion Press, 2006). See http://www.abcd institute.org/publications/related/.

22. Executive Office of the President, *Up from Dependency: A New National Public Assistance Strategy,* report to the president (Washington, DC: GPO, 1986), 12–14.

23. U.S. Department of Health and Human Services, Administration for Children and Families, TANF Financial Data, Table A, Spending from Federal TANF Grant in FY 2008.

24. John Kretzmann and John L. McKnight, with Sarah Dobrowolski and Deborah Puntenney, *Discovering Community Power: A Guide to Mobilizing Local Assets and Your Organization's Capacity* (Evanston, IL: Asset-Based Community Development Institute, School of Education and Social Policy, Northwestern University, 2005), http://www.abcdinstitute.org.

25. *NAACP v. Alabama,* 357 U.S. 449 (1958).

■ Chapter 6: Awakening the Power of Families and Neighborhoods

26. Alexis de Tocqueville, *Democracy in America*, vol. II (1840; New York: Vintage Books, 1945), 114.

27. Ibid, 118.

▓ *Resources*

▓ *Pioneers: People Who Are Creating Abundant Communities*

Minette Bauer
Youth Advocate Programs

Minette and her group have created a way to circle "youth-at-risk" with a supportive group of neighborhood people. They provide a positive alternative to the criminal justice system.
http://www.yapinc.org

Bill Berkowitz
Author of *Community Dreams*
Community Tool Box

Bill is a pioneer in understanding the power of relationships as community-building tools; his book *Community Dreams* remains the best eye-opener regarding possibilities for local invention.
http://ctb.ku.edu

Paul Born
Tamarack: An Institute for Community Engagement

This group uses community building and cooperative strategies to get at the root causes of poverty in cities across Canada and New Zealand. They are research based and engage people at the lower

levels and margins of society to develop new thinking for a difficult and stubborn issue. They are getting some amazing results.
http://tamarackcommunity.ca

Gordon Cunningham and Alison Mathie
Coady International Institute

Gordon and Alison, based at St. Francis Xavier University in Antigonish, Nova Scotia, Canada, have become leaders of an international movement focusing on the power of local relationships and assets in the village development process.
http://www.coady.stfx.ca

Jim Diers
Neighbor Power

Jim led the City of Seattle's neighborhood department to support neighborhood invention and problem solving. His book, *Neighbor Power: Building Community the Seattle Way,* describes the diversity of initiatives that neighbors undertake when government supports rather than controls or ignores their efforts.
http://home.comcast.net/~jimdiers/index.html

Tim Dutton and April Doner
Sarasota County Openly Plans for Excellence (SCOPE)

Tim and April are members of a citizen engagement organization in Sarasota, Florida, where their leadership in focusing the community on the importance of local relationships and assets has resulted in a climate of invention.
http://www.scopexcel.org

Joe Erpenbeck
Hamilton County Developmental Disabilities Services ABCD Group
Sandra Nahornoff
Project Friendship Society

Joe, in Cincinnati, and Sandra, in Prince George, British Columbia, Canada, are masters at creating local initiatives that draw marginal and labeled people back into neighborhood relationships.
Joe Erpenbeck: http://www.hamiltondds.org/Resources/ABCD.aspx
Sandra Nahornoff: http://www.projectfriendship.com

Al Etmanski
Planned Lifetime Advocacy Network (PLAN)
Philia

Al is a leading social inventor in Canada who has learned how to create effective associations that support labeled people outside service systems. We can all learn from his explorations of effective new problem-solving networks.

Al Etmanski: http://www.plan.ca
Philia: http://www.philia.ca

The Faculty of the Asset-Based Community Development Institute

This is an international group of creative practitioners of an asset-based approach to community building. Their biographies and contact information are on their website.

http://www.ABCDInstitute.org

Wayne Helgason and Glen Cochrane
Social Planning Council of Winnipeg

These two Canadian First Nation leaders have helped renew the traditional knowledge that powerful nations are gift centered.

http://www.spcw.mb.ca

Ann Livingston
Vancouver Area Network of Drug Users (VANDA)

Ann has learned how to protect a supportive association from lapsing into becoming one more service agency. Her association has provided opportunities for addicted people to create useful, productive neighborhood initiatives and relationships.

http://www.vandu.org

Mike Mather
Broadway United Methodist Church

As the pastor of an inner-city congregation in Indianapolis, Mike has invented and supported new initiatives to create productive neighborhood friendships.

http://www.broadwayumc.org

■ **Allison Pinto**

Central-Cocoanut Neighborhood Scavenger Hunters

> Allison is leading the way toward new understandings of the crea-
> tivity and inventiveness of a neighborhood's young children. The
> Scavengers are enabling new roles for children to be community
> builders.
>
> *http://centralcocoanutsarasota.neighborlogs.com*

Jackie Reed

Every Block a Village, Westside Health Authority

> Jackie has led the organizing effort of EBV on Chicago's West Side.
> The organization creates unique webs of relationships among
> neighbors whose mutual support creates amazing opportunities.
>
> *http://www.healthauthority.org/everyblock.html*

Olivia Saunders

> Olivia is an associate professor of economics at the College of the
> Bahamas. She is a voice for an economics based on abundance
> rather than scarcity. Her thinking is grounded in her deep commit-
> ment to find an alternative to the modern forms of colonialism.
> Her efforts are directed to exposing and celebrating the gifts inher-
> ent in individuals, communities, and nations. Both are refreshing
> to find in the academy.
>
> *If you want to contact Olivia, please let us know (pbi@att.net).*

Lois Smidt

Beyond Welfare

> Lois has led a group of neighbors in Ames, Iowa, in creating an
> open door for people leaving the welfare system. The group under-
> stands that their hospitality includes money, friends, and a new
> meaning for life.
>
> *http://www.beyondwelfare.org*

Judith Snow

Inclusion Network

> Judith has been a key inventor of Circles of Support, now an inter-
> national movement creating new community relationships around
> excluded and marginalized people.
>
> *http://www.inclusion.com/assnow.html*

Dr. Frances Strickland

Frances is innovating new approaches for people in politics. The wife of the governor of Ohio, Ted Strickland, she uses this platform to build cooperation in the human service and educational system world. Her message and way of engaging others always affirms the capacities of citizens and people at the local level.
If you want to contact Frances, please let us know (pbi@att.net).

Collette Thompson
A Small Group

Collette is a connector by nature, cares deeply about our children, and is inventing ways in which neighborhoods and communities become competent. She has helped create A Small Group, a network of citizens engaged in caring for their community.
http://www.asmallgroup.net

Ray Thompson
Thompson Community Relations Group

Ray has fashioned a new institutional role: the *school–community connector*. His innovative experiments creating new, two-way relationships between a local school and its surrounding neighborhood are groundbreaking.
http://www.thompsoncrg.com
http://www.catalyst-chicago.org/news/index.php?item=2461&cat=23

Marian Tompson
La Leche League

Marian founded La Leche League, an association of women supporting family life in their own community. The movement is now worldwide and growing in aspiration and influence.
http://www.llli.org

Paul Uhlig
Project Access

If you want to see the face of authentic health care reform, study the work that Paul is doing. He is a thoracic surgeon in practice but is a force for choosing health over disease. He has demonstrated the healing effects of collaborative care, and the practical and curative effects of focusing on people's gifts and capacities.

http://www.projectaccess.net
puhlig@kumc.edu

Brighde Vallely

Brighde is a peace builder in Northern Ireland. She has given her life to becoming a bridge for groups who believed that their history and stories made connection impossible. She completely embodies the power of a door-to-door, patient, persistent, person-to-person strategy for changing the world.

corini@btconnect.com

Sarah van Gelder
Yes! Magazine

This magazine and website cover an elegant scope of wisdom and insight, from large policy questions like the restructuring of our financial system to what individuals and small associations are doing to transform their neighborhoods and thereby the world. An indispensable source for those who care for the well-being of us all.

http://www.yesmagazine.org

Louise van Rhyn
Symphonia

Louise and those around her are engaged in nation building in South Africa. They embody a relationship-based and collaborative stance to creating the future. If there is a country in the world that will show us that a society based on compassion and accountability is possible, it will be South Africa. Louise will be in the forefront of creating that possibility.

http://www.symphonia.net

Bob Woodson
Center for Neighborhood Enterprise

For decades, Bob has led initiatives in low-income minority communities that demonstrate how local community relationships are the ultimate source of power and empowerment.

http://www.cneonline.org

■ *Website*

Visit our website: http://www.abundantcommunity.com.

This is a site whose first commitment is to action.

A place to find others who are like you or aren't.

We are committed to learning and to supporting the movement toward local living. It is a site based on welcoming, gift-mindedness, strong association, and communities that work.

We have created a website for and with you. There are four parts of the site to check out:

Toolkit. A toolkit to help you put these ideas to work. This includes methods for getting started, discovering gifts, making connections, learning from each other, and tracking the connections.

Where It Is Working. Studies, research, and transformational efforts under way. Efforts to create a new narrative for our communities based on gifts and hospitality.

Commentary. Blogs and podcasts from John McKnight and Peter Block. Commentaries from a wide network of friends who are changing our thinking and the world. Space for the thoughts and experiences of connectors, activists, and citizens. Book reviews. Especially ideas that you might not have discovered yet.

Events. Abundant Community gatherings. Local meetings of people interested in these ideas. National calendar of presentations, workshops, and meetings.

We want to hear from you. Go to the website:
http://www.abundantcommunity.com.

■ *References*

The Abundant Community is a book born of our experience and way of thinking. Many published and unpublished writings have influenced our thinking over the years. We include in this list those that have most helped us to form the ideas we have given voice to in this book, as well as a couple of our own previous works. Publications from which we have quoted directly and sources from which we learned facts not commonly known are cited in the "Notes" section.

Berry, Wendell. *The Unsettling of America: Culture and Agriculture*. Rev. ed. San Francisco: Sierra Club Books, 1996. Originally published 1977.

Block, Peter. *Community: The Structure of Belonging*. San Francisco: Berrett-Koehler Publishers, 2008.

de Tocqueville, Alexis. *Democracy in America*, vol. II. New York: Vintage Books, 1945. Originally published in two vols. 1835, 1984.

Green, Mike, with Henry Moore and John O'Brien. *ABCD in Action: When People Care Enough to Act*. Toronto: Inclusion Press, 2006. See also http://www.abcdinstitute.org/publications/related.

Illich, Ivan. *Deschooling Society. World Perspectives*, vol. 44. New York: Harper & Row, 1971.

————. *Medical Nemesis: The Expropriation of Health*. New York: Pantheon Books, 1976.

————. *Toward a History of Needs*. New York: Pantheon Books, 1978.

Jacobs, Jane. *The Death and Life of Great American Cities*. Reprint ed. New York: Modern Library, 1993. Originally published 1961. See also *Dark Age Ahead* (New York: Random House, 2004) and "Healthy Cities, Urban Theory, and Design: The Power of Jane Jacobs," http://bss.sfsu.edu/pamuk/urban/.

Kaplan, Jeffrey. "The Gospel of Consumption: And the Better Future We Left Behind." *Orion*, May/June 2008. http://www.orionmagazine.org/index.php/articles/article/2962 (accessed April 29, 2009).

Kohn, Alfie. *No Contest: The Case Against Competition*. Rev. ed. Boston: Houghton Mifflin, 1992.

————. *Punished by Rewards: The Trouble with Gold Stars, Incentive Plans, A's, Praise, and Other Bribes*. Rev. ed. New York: Mariner Books, 1999. See also http://www.alfiekohn.org.

Kretzmann, John P., and John L. McKnight. *Building Communities from the Inside Out: A Path toward Finding and Mobilizing a Community's Assets*. Evanston, IL: The Asset-Based Community Development Institute, 1993. Distributed by ACTA Publications, Chicago, IL.

Kretzmann, John P., and John L. McKnight, with Sarah Dobrowolski and Deborah Puntenney. *Discovering Community Power: A Guide to Mobilizing Local Assets and Your Organization's Capacity.* Evanston, IL: Asset-Based Community Development Institute, Northwestern University, 2005. Available at http://www.abcdinstitute.org/docs/kelloggabcd.pdf (accessed January 10, 2010).

McKnight, John L. *The Careless Society: Community and Its Counterfeits.* New York: Basic Books, 1995.

Nouwen, Henri J. M. *Reaching Out: The Three Movements of the Spiritual Life.* New York: Doubleday, 1975.

Putnam, Robert D. *Bowling Alone: The Collapse and Revival of American Community.* New York: Simon & Schuster, 2000. See also http://www.bowling alone.com.

———. *Making Democracy Work: Civic Traditions in Modern Italy.* Princeton, NJ: Princeton University Press, 1992.

Robbins, Lionel. *An Essay on the Nature and Significance of Economic Science.* London: Macmillan, 1932; 2nd ed. 1935. http://www.scribd.com/doc/142 42989/An-Essay-on-the-Nature-and-Significance-of-Economic-Science-Lionel-Robbins-.

Sampson, Robert J. Papers derived from the ongoing "Project on Human Development in Chicago Neighborhoods." University of Michigan, Inter-university Consortium for Political and Social Research. http://www.icpsr .umich.edu/PHDCN/publications.html.

Schumacher, E. F. *Small Is Beautiful: Economics as if People Mattered.* Paper ed. Vancouver, BC: Hartley & Marks, 1999. Originally published 1973.

▦ *Acknowledgments*

FOR HALF A CENTURY, thousands of people in hundreds of neighborhoods have taught me about community. In the last fifteen years, I have been especially informed by my community colleagues in the Circle of Friends from the Asset-Based Community Building Institute at Northwestern University. The institute's codirector, Jody Kretzmann, has been the creative, committed fellow traveler who has made my community journey possible.

In memoriam, there is one other friend and colleague who holds a special place: Ivan Illich. His vision of the authentic community and the dangers of technology has informed and guided me through all my later years.

John L. McKnight
Evanston, Illinois
January 2010

I CANNOT IMAGINE writing a book without the support, intelligence, and skill of our developmental editor, Leslie Stephen. She got in early on this book; met often with John and me, which enriched our conversation; and stayed with it through the health challenges of her own life.

In many ways, this book is written out of concern for the next generation. I am grateful to Ellen and David Krikorian for their presence, love, and enlivening effect on my life. They give me a glimpse into the thinking, desires, beauty, and talents of under-twenties, and I know they will do a better job of creating a world that works for all than my generation. Corny as this is, I also want to acknowledge the gift of my grandchildren, Leyland, Gracie, and Auggie Reilly. They care for the planet, all its living creatures, and each other. They are a source of constant joy—can I show you some pictures?

I publish with Berrett-Koehler primarily because of Steve Piersanti. He, along with the entire BK staff, has great integrity and commitment to a just society. Plus Steve is a genius in understanding the marketplace and has a super editor's instinct for knowing what a book wants to become.

I want to thank others who made the book work. The four reviewers—Ellyn Kerr, Rebecca Maillet, Josh O'Conner, and Frappa Stout—were unusually attentive to the book, supported its intention, and were quite helpful. Thanks to Elissa Rabellino for the copyediting, Dianne Platner and Rick Wilson for production, and Leigh McLellan for the design of the book.

Finally, appreciation to Jennifer and Heather for demonstrating that my so-so parenting was not a limiting factor on the fine human beings they have become. As always, thanks to Maggie, my most trusted and valued comrade in all work endeavors; to Collette, who brings passion, love, and great instinct to this impossible project of building communities; and to Cathy, again, for it all.

Peter Block
Cincinnati, Ohio
January 2010

☷ Index

abundance, 52, 83–111, *See also* gifts; culture of, 91–96; lives of cooperation and, 14–15; making gifts visible, 120–122; properties and capacities, 67–68; structure of, 65–70; tenets of, 66–67

abundant communities, 5, 43–44, 65–82; community-friendly policies, 99–100; cooperation, 86–87; cultural traits, 92–96; and democracy, 109–111; example of, 145–148; fallibility, 88–90; forgiveness, 87–88; generosity and kindness, 85–86; hospitality, 78–79; Listening Tables, 101; mystery, 90–91

addiction prevention and recovery groups, 126

advisory community support groups, 126

aggregate deficiencies, 41–42

aging, and the community way, 38–39

Alcoholics Anonymous, 20, 75

Alessio, N., 145–148

Alinsky, S., 78

animal care groups, 127

anticrime groups, 127

Arendt, H., 88

arranged marriage, disappearance of, 58

Asset-Based Community Development Institute, faculty at, 155

associational connections, benefits of, 123–124

associational life, 71–78

associations, 83, 116, 119; associations of associations, 131; and connected gifts, 123–124; defined, 5, 131; forms of, 73–74, 126–129; power of, 125–126; properties and capacities, 72–73; purpose of, 81; systems compared to, 75

automated human functions, 32–33

barter exchange, creating, 122

Barton, J., 145–148

basic functions, provided by systems, 10

Bauer, M., 153

Berkowitz, B., 153

Berry, W., 13–14

Beyond Welfare, 156

Bikers Against Child Abuse (BACA), 74–75

Block, P., 159

blue ribbon, 107

book clubs, 77–78

boredom, 61

Born, P., 153–154

Bowling Alone (Putnam), 20

Broadway United Methodist Church, Indianapolis IN, 71, 108–109, 134, 155

business organizations/support groups, 127

capacities: of an abundant community, 84; professionalizing, colonizing dimension of, 40; communities, 67–68; of a competent community, 83–84

care, 4, 24; aggregate deficiencies, 41–42; converting into service, 37–42; enslavement to debt, 50, 53–54; loss of, 55–56; outsourcing to professionals, 36–42

caring for the whole, 87

carpooling, 121

Center for Neighborhood Enterprise, 158

Central-Cocoanut Neighborhood Scavenger Hunters, 156

certifiable standards, 30

charitable groups and drives, 127

charity, 85

child care, and the elderly/retired, 122

children, 3–4; well-being of, 21

children's clothes exchange, 120

choice, and associations, 77–78

citizen: defined, 7; shift to consumer, 7–25

citizen economy, 96–98; and community competence, 98; developing, 97–98

citizen engagement, 107

citizen way, 14–15; contrast between consumer way and, 15–18

civic events groups, 127

Coady International Institute, 154

Cochrane, G., 155

commodification, 39

community, 5: competent, 55; defined, 131; incompetent, 55

community abundance, *See* abundance; abundant communities

community connectors, *See* connectors

community competence, 5, 78, 81; collective gifts/sorrow as community

knowledge, 69; and neighborhoods, 57; use of term, 10

community connectors: characteristics of, 133; and competent communities, 133; defined, 132; finding our way into the heart of the community, 140–141; hiring, 132; role of, 132–133; table for, 133–137

community culture, 64; building, 117

Community Dreams (Berkowitz), 153

community functions, *See* neighborhood necessities

community gardens, 24

community life, and order and structure, 81

community possibilities, 25

community structure, 76; invisible structures of, 81–82

Community Tool Box, 153

community way: and aging, 38–39; use of term, 5

competent communities, 5, 55, 78, 81; associational life, 71–78; gift-mindedness, 70–71; and neighborhoods, 57; personal information, sharing, 69–70; properties and capacities, 67–68, 83–91; self-organization, 74–75

competent community, 55; capacities of, 83–91

competition: cost of, 86; fallacy of, 86–87

connections, making, 142–143

connectors: characteristics of, 133; and competent communities, 133; defined, 132; finding our way into the heart of the community, 140–141; hiring, 132; power of, 132–148; role of, 132–133; table for, 133–137

Connectors' Table, 134–137; associations, connecting, 136–137; individual gifts, connecting, 135–136

consumer culture, power of, 49

consumer economy: development of, 28; saving in, 54

consumer model, fallacy of, 62
consumer society: and community wisdom, 63; full effects of, understanding, 26; life in, 13–14; promise of, 9, 42; supply of basic functions in, 10
consumer way, 11–14
consumer world, 46–62; paying the price for living in, 62
consumerism, 46; core beliefs, 47–49; cost to society, 49–54; and gift-giving satisfaction, 84; invasion of work and the system way, 48–49; purchasing power, and the good life, 47–48; and the system way, 48
consumption: limits of, 9–25; lives of scarcity and, 11–14; social cost of, 9–10
consumption dependency, 51
cooperation, 86–87
cooperative local relationships, 100
credit unions, 105
crime, and aggregate deficiencies, 41–42
cultural groups, 127
cultural traits of abundant communities, 92–96
cultural wisdom, 63–64
culture: of abundance, 91–96; choice of, 15–18
Cunningham, G., 154
customer satisfaction, 62

Davis, J. J., 17
de Tocqueville, A., 75, 124–125
dead air, 94–95
debt, enslavement to, 50, 53–54
debt burden, 50
democracy, and abundant communities, 109–111
Democracy in America (de Tocqueville), 124–125
denial, 44–45
depersonalization, 32, 69
Descartes, R., 9
devaluation of the personal, 55
Diers, J., 154

disability/special needs groups, 127
Discovering Community Power, 103–104
dissatisfaction: origin of, 27–29; persistence of, 27; successful marketing of, 50–51
Doner, A., 154
Dutton, T., 154

economy, 3
Edgerton, J. E., 17
education, and privatization, 52
education groups, 127
elements of satisfaction, 2–4
enterprising economy, 22–23
entrepreneurs, shared insights from, 121
environment, 3, 22
environmental groups, 127
environmental impact statement, 102
Erpenbeck, J., 154
Etmanski, A., 155
Every Block a Village, 156

Faculty of the Asset-Based Community Development Institute, 155
fallibility, 88–90; accepting, 43–44
family function: loss of, 57–58; and neighborhoods, 57
family support groups, 127
feuds, 87
food, 3, 23–24
Ford, H., 47
forgiveness, 87–88
free market, 48

generosity, in abundant communities, 85–86
gift giving, 4, 56; and satisfaction, 84
gift-powered practice, 75, 80–81
gifts, 83, 116, 140–141; making visible, 120–122; of neighborhoods, 119–120; power of, 122–123
goldbricking, 93
good life: and large systems, 48; and purchasing power, 47–48

government, and privatization, 52
grants, 103

Hamilton County Developmental Dis-
    abilities Services ABCD Group, 154
Harges, D., 134
health, 2, 20
health advocacy and fitness groups, 128
health care, and privatization, 52
health exchange, 122
Helgason, W., 155
heritage groups, 128
Highlander Research and Education
    Center, 85
hollowness, 57
Hoover, H., 27
hospitality, 83, 113, 116, 119; and abun-
    dant communities, 78–81; compassion
    of, 5; defined, 78–79; friendship and
    trust, 79–80; gift-powered practice,
    80–81

Illich, I., 91
immortality, selling, 43
Inclusion Network, 156
incompetent community, 55
individual vs. communal properties and
    capacities, 72–73
individuation, 69

Jacobs, J., 19–20

Kaplan, J., 17, 27, 49, 53, 59
Kellogg, W. K., 59
Kettering, C., 17
kindness, in abundant communities,
    84–85
Kohn, A., 86
Kretzmann, J., 163

La Leche League, 157
Listening Tables, 101
Livingston, A., 155
local purchasing policy shift, 104–105

local social relationships, as health
    sources, 20
local stewardship, and common outdoor
    neighborhood space, 22
lost satisfaction of neighboring, 56–57

Making Democracy Work (Putnam), 22
management: purpose of, 32; and systems,
    30–32
management science, 30
mass customization, 30
Mather, M., 108, 155
Mathie, A., 154
McKnight, J., 159
medical system, 20
men's groups, 128
mentoring groups, 128
money, understanding the limits of, 123
Moore, H., 101
mutual support groups, 122, 128; creating,
    122
mystery, 40, 90–91

Nahornoff, S., 154
nature, marginalization of, 49–51
need saturation, 17
Neighbor Power, 154
neighborhood: cost of good life to, 54–57;
    defined, 5; devaluation of the per-
    sonal, 55; forum, 121; impact state-
    ment, 102; improvement groups, 128;
    jobs, 105; keeping money in, 104–105;
    loss of care, 55–56; lost satisfaction
    of neighboring, 56–57; outsiders in,
    138–139; security form, 122
neighborhood necessities, 18–24; care, 24;
    enterprising economy, 22–23; environ-
    ment/land, 22; food, 23–24; health,
    20; safety, 19–20; security, 19–20;
    well-being of children, 21
Nouwen, H., 113

outsiders: beyond community borders,
    139; in the neighborhood, 138–139;

reluctance to approach neighbors, 139–140

outsourcing of care to professionals, 36–42

Overeaters Anonymous, 20

peacemakers, 122

perfection, selling, 43

personal limitations, 37-38

Philia, 155

Pinto, A., 156

pioneers, lessons from, 117–118

Planned Lifetime Advocacy Network (PLAN), 155

possibilities list, 142

potluck dinners, 87, 121

practice, 141–142

privacy, 40, 69

privatization, growth of, 52

professional solution-mystification, 39–41

professionalization, defined, 36

Project Access, 157–158

Project Friendship Society, 154

properties, of communities, 67–68

prosperity, 97

psychiatry, defined, 36

public interest, argument for privatizing, 52

purchasing power: and the good life, 47–48; and the system way, 48

Putnam, R., 20, 22

quality time, 106

recovery groups, 126

recreation groups, 128

Reed, J., 156

residents' associations, 128

Relationships: and associations, 81; cooperative local, 100; local social, as health sources, 20; neighborhoods of, 55; to order, 77; and systems, 33, 81; utilitarian, 32–33

Robbins, L., 97

romantic marriage, development of, 58

safety, 2–3, 19–20

Sampson, R. J., 19

sanctification of needs, 28–29

Sarasota County Openly Plans for Excellence (SCOPE), 154

satisfaction, 35; and associations, 129–130; as collective occurrence, 57; customer, 62; elements of, 2–4; fallibility, accepting, 43–44; and gift giving, 84; limits of, 65; spin and denial, 44–45; suffering, inevitability of, 44

satisfied life, choosing, 64

Saturn (General Motors), 33–34

Saunders, O., 156

savings, commitment to, 54

scale, 29

school system, and family/community functions, 28

school–community connector, 157

Schumacher, E. F., 96

Schumacher Society, 98

Schwartz, D., 91

science/engineering, and standards, 30

security, 2–3, 19–20

Self-chosen order, in community space, 76

self-expression, and satisfaction, 84

self-organization, 74–75

service clubs, 128

service economy, development of, 28

service-seeking family, 16

shared transportation, 121

sharing personal information, 69–70

silence, as cultural trait of abundant communities, 94–95

Small Group, 157

Smidt, L., 148, 156

Snow, J., 156

social cause/advocacy issue groups, 129

social fabric, 81

social groups, 129

Social Planning Council of Winnipeg, 155

social systems, *See* systems

special needs groups, 127

spectators, and thought, 60–61

spin, 44–45

standards, 30

statemanship, 87

storytelling, as cultural trait of abundant communities, 95–96

Strickland, F., 157

Strickland, T., 157

suffering, inevitability of, 44

surprise, loss of capacity for, 60–61

Symphonia, 158

system life, 13, 74, 82

systems: associations compared to, 75; certainty and scale, 31; counterfeit promise of, 43; growth of, 29–36; and management, 30–32; and relationships, 33; services offered by, 24

Tamarack: An Institute for Community Engagement, 153–154

Temporary Assistance for Needy Families (TANF), 103

Thompson, C., 157

Thompson Community Relations Group, 157

Thompson, R., 157

thought, loss of capacity for, 60–61

time, as cultural trait of abundant communities, 92–94

Tompson, M., 157

training, and systems, 34

trust: and friendship, 79–80; as code word for loyalty, 80

Truth and Reconciliation Commission (South Africa), 87–88

tutor list, 120

Uhlig, P., 157–158

uniformity, and systems, 30–31

universal properties, 4–5; abundance, community of, 5; association, presence of, 4; gift giving, 4; hospitality, compassion of, 5

urban design, and community connections, 10

usury, 53

utilitarian relationships, 32–33

Vallely, B., 158

van Gelder, S., 158

van Rhyn, L., 158

Vancouver Area Network of Drug Users (VANDA), 155

veterans' groups, 129

viable local economy, building, 102–103

volunteerism, 76

well-being of children, 21

wired life, 57–61; boredom, 61; capacity for thought and surprise, atrophy of, 60–61; family function, loss of, 57–58; work and consumption, 58–60

witnessing, 95

women's groups, 129

Woodson, B., 158

workday, 59

Yeats, W. B., 138

Yes! Magazine, 158

Youth Advocate Programs, 153

youth groups, 129

▦ *About the Authors*

JOHN L. MCKNIGHT was raised a traveling Ohioan, having lived in seven neighborhoods and small towns in the eighteen years before he left to attend Northwestern University, in Evanston, Illinois. There, he had the good fortune to be educated by a faculty dedicated to preparing students for effective citizenship. He graduated into the U.S. Navy, where he had three years of "postgraduate" education in Asia during the Korean War.

McKnight returned to Chicago and began working for several activist organizations, including the Chicago Commission for Human Relations, the first municipal civil rights agency. There he learned the Alinsky trade called *community organizing*. This was followed by the directorship of the Illinois American Civil Liberties Union, where he organized local chapters throughout the state.

When John Kennedy was elected president, McKnight was recruited into the federal government, where he worked with a new agency that created the affirmative action program. Later, he was appointed the Midwest director of the United States Commission on Civil Rights, where he worked with local civil rights and neighborhood organizations.

In 1969, McKnight's alma mater, Northwestern University, invited him to return and help initiate a new department called the Center for Urban Affairs. This was a group of interdisciplinary faculty doing research designed to support urban change agents and progressive urban policy. McKnight's

■

Peter Block and John McKnight

photo by Ward Mailliard

appointment was an act of heroism on the part of the university, as it gave him a tenured professorship, though he had only a bachelor's degree.

While at the center and its successor, the Institute for Policy Research, McKnight and a few of his colleagues focused their research on urban neighborhoods. The best-known result of this work was the formulation of an understanding of neighborhoods focused on the usefulness of local resources, capacities, and relationships. This work was documented in a guide titled *Building Communities from the Inside Out,* describing an approach to community building that became a major development strategy practiced in North and South America, Europe, Africa, Asia, and Australia. As an aside, it was during this time that McKnight was one of the trainers of Barack Obama as he learned the skills of community organizing.

McKnight is also the author of *The Careless Society,* a classic critique of professionalized social services and a celebration of communities' ability to heal themselves from within.

Currently, McKnight has joined Peter Block in practical explorations of how communities become "villages" with the capacity to raise their children.

PETER BLOCK was born in Chicago and spent most of his early years in the Midwest. After college, he went to New Jersey and was involved in the early days of creating the field of organization development. This entailed some years at Exxon Research and Engineering Company and then the formation of a consulting firm with Tony Petrella. Marvin Weisbord joined in 1971, and the firm did pretty well until, Block says, "we all got into our sixties and either retired or moved in other directions."

In 1980, Block started Designed Learning, a training company that offers workshops based on the ideas in his books. It still thrives and works to help staff people in organizations to have more influence and impact.

In 1995, Block got involved with city government and city managers through conferences held by the Innovations Group based in Florida. This led to his interest in building community, which has been his obsession ever since. Block met McKnight at a community conference convened by Police Chief Mike Butler in Longmont, Colorado. This is where their common view of the world became obvious to both of them, which eventually culminated in writing this book.

Block has written seven other books, including *Flawless Consulting, The Empowered Manager, Stewardship, Freedom and Accountability* (with Peter Koestenbaum), *The Answer to How Is Yes*, and *Community: The Structure of Belonging*.

The community work is now centered in Cincinnati, Ohio, where Block has been a citizen since 1998. He is engaged in developing a civic engagement network called A Small Group, plus a series of other projects working on building the capacity of this urban community to value its gifts and see its own possibility.

■ *Designed Learning*

Designed Learning is a training and consulting group that offers work-shops based on the ideas and books of Peter Block. Through a variety of innovative ideas and technologies, we help our client organizations support their learning objectives. We offer programs on Flawless Consulting and the Six Conversations That Matter. These are hands-on experiences that help organizations build capacity and develop people to achieve more successful, more meaningful work. To learn more about our workshops and consulting services, contact

Bill Brewer
bbrewer@designedlearning.com
Phone: 513.524.2227 or 866.770.2227
Email: info@designedlearning.com
Designed Learning (**www.designedlearning.com**)

■ *ABCD*

The Asset-Based Community Development Institute at Northwestern University is codirected by John McKnight. We provide training, consultations, and publications about effective community building using the abundant resources of local neighborhoods. Our website is **www.abcd institute.org**.

■ *A Small Group*

A Small Group offers a model to communities and organizations to hold conversations that matter. Our vision is a world where citizens take ownership for their communities; our mission is to equip citizens with the resources needed to cocreate restorative communities that take advantage of the gifts of everyone. We use methodologies developed by Peter Block to promote authentic dialogue designed to change the narrative of a community. To learn the details of A Small Group, visit our website: **www.asmallgroup.net**.

AMERICAN PLANNING ASSOCIATION

The American Planning Association is an independent, nonprofit educational organization that provides leadership in the development of vital communities by advocating excellence in community planning, promoting education and citizen empowerment, and providing the tools and support necessary to meet the challenges of growth and change.

APA's more than 42,000 members include professional planners, officials, educators, students, and other individuals interested in making great communities happen. APA members can be found in all 50 states and in 75 countries.

Membership
Not only do members become part of a large national network, but local chapters connect members close to home. Divisions bring together members with similar special interests. And member benefits include discounts on select publications and training opportunities and a members-only job service.

Events
APA hosts a number of events annually, including educational conferences, workshops, lectures, and symposiums. APA's National Planning Conference is the nation's premier planning event, which brings together more than 5,000 planners annually for learning and networking opportunities.

Outreach
APA recognizes the importance of planners and planning both nationally and internationally through national awards and designation programs. The Global Planners Network brings together a network of national planning associations to share knowledge and build capacities for planning across the globe.

Tracking current legislative initiatives and advocating for good planning practices on Capitol Hill is part of the advocacy work done by APA on behalf of its members.

Resources
APA's research projects provide practical, up-to-date information about best practices in urban and regional planning. A variety of printed and online publications explore planning in all its breadth and depth.

APA Planners Press
Planners Press, APA's book imprint, publishes titles of interest to practitioners, researchers, and the general public, with the aim of stimulating readers, creating an engaged citizenry, and influencing policy development—all by telling the many stories of planning.

Employment
Jobs Online connects APA members and prospective employers. This members-only benefit offers an extensive database of jobs and candidates in planning and allied professional fields.

APAPlanningBooks.com
Looking for a planning publication? The online bookstore carries planning and allied professional publications ranging from day-to-day manuals to think pieces.

American Planning Association
Making Great Communities Happen

■ *Be Connected*

Visit Our Website

Go to www.bkconnection.com to read exclusive previews and excerpts of new books, find detailed information on all Berrett-Koehler titles and authors, browse subject-area libraries of books, and get special discounts.

Subscribe to Our Free E-Newsletter

Be the first to hear about new publications, special discount offers, exclusive articles, news about bestsellers, and more! Get on the list for our free e-newsletter by going to www.bkconnection.com.

Get Quantity Discounts

Berrett-Koehler books are available at quantity discounts for orders of ten or more copies. Please call us toll-free at (800) 929-2929 or email us at bkp.orders@aidcvt.com.

Host a Reading Group

For tips on how to form and carry on a book reading group in your workplace or community, see our website at www.bkconnection.com.

Join the BK Community

Thousands of readers of our books have become part of the "BK Community" by participating in events featuring our authors, reviewing draft manuscripts of forthcoming books, spreading the word about their favorite books, and supporting our publishing program in other ways.

If you would like to join the BK Community, please contact us at **bkcommunity@bkpub.com**.